PARENT PARTNERSHIP IN THE PRIMARY SCHOOL

Parent partnership is a powerful tool in maximising children's outcomes in the primary school. *Parent Partnership in the Primary School* will enable you to evaluate your current practice in this crucial area of school life and provides practical, easy-to-follow steps to plan and deliver improvements successfully. The book explores five key principles for leaders, managers, teachers, support staff, volunteers and governors to focus on in their drive to engage all parents and carers as genuine partners in their child's learning.

Pulling together recommendations from a wide range of international sources, this book builds upon 20 years of research evidence highlighting the importance of parent involvement and engagement. Bishop also brings his own broad experiences from a 32-year career in primary education, as a teacher, school leader, consultant and trainer, to bear on the many challenges facing schools as they seek to welcome, encourage, inform and support those whose children they educate.

Detailed case studies from six carefully selected schools, with which Bishop has worked as a consultant, exemplify some of the most successful techniques and programmes currently in use to facilitate parent partnership. Suggestions for further reading are included, and for leaders and managers there is an easy-to-use audit tool to support their strategic thinking and school improvement activity.

Nigel Bishop is a former primary headteacher who provides training and consultancy to schools, primarily on using the Pupil Premium. He is also a person-centred counsellor and school governor. His experience and enthusiasm allow him to equip those who learn with him to continue moving mountains.

PARENT PARTNERSHIP IN THE PRIMARY SCHOOL

A practical guide for school leaders and other key staff

Nigel Bishop

LONDON AND NEW YORK

Designed cover image: © Getty Images

First edition published 2023
by Routledge
4 Park Square, Milton Park, Abingdon, Oxon, OX14 4RN

and by Routledge
605 Third Avenue, New York, NY 10158

Routledge is an imprint of the Taylor & Francis Group, an informa business

© 2023 Nigel Bishop

The right of Nigel Bishop to be identified as author of this work has been asserted in accordance with sections 77 and 78 of the Copyright, Designs and Patents Act 1988.

All rights reserved. No part of this book may be reprinted or reproduced or utilised in any form or by any electronic, mechanical, or other means, now known or hereafter invented, including photocopying and recording, or in any information storage or retrieval system, without permission in writing from the publishers.

Trademark notice: Product or corporate names may be trademarks or registered trademarks, and are used only for identification and explanation without intent to infringe.

British Library Cataloguing-in-Publication Data
A catalogue record for this book is available from the British Library

ISBN: 978-1-032-14037-7 (hbk)
ISBN: 978-1-032-14039-1 (pbk)
ISBN: 978-1-003-23207-0 (ebk)

DOI: 10.4324/9781003232070

Typeset in Interstate
by Apex CoVantage, LLC

Access the Support Material: https://www.routledge.com/9781032140377

CONTENTS

1. Research evidence: what recent research says about the effects of parental engagement on pupils' learning — 1

2. A suggested model for parental engagement: unpacking Desforges and Abouchaar's model, with suggestions as to how it might inform a primary school's strategic thinking — 18

3. Principles for practice in parental involvement and engagement: suggested characteristics, behaviours and attitudes that could support successful parent partnership, when used by practitioners and parents alike — 36

4. Case studies: the methodology for selecting the schools, collecting evidence about their parent partnership practice and presenting it in an organised form — 48

5. Respect: ways in which schools seek to show respect to parents, and encourage respect in return — 53

6. Knowledge: the extent to which the school knows the nature and quality of its parent partnership work, the needs of its parents, and the steps it takes to encourage parents to know what the school offers and how they can access and contribute to it — 64

7. Understanding and empathy: ways in which each school's staff demonstrate that they listen to what is really being said, share their own related experiences appropriately and empower parents to take ownership of their strengths and areas for growth — 74

8. Relationship: the links and bonds that are created between the school and its parents, leading to clear communication, thoughtful responses to ideas and shared decision making — 83

9. Trust: the reciprocal bond that arguably builds up through application of the previous four principles in the school's dealings with its parents, and which may need to be nurtured over time if is to be sustained — 94

10 **Conclusions and next steps for schools: what are we to make of all this? What does it mean for my educational practice? Where might we go next as a school?** 111

Appendix 117

1 Research evidence

What recent research says about the effects of parental engagement on pupils' learning

Whenever schools seek to improve the education they offer, a useful starting point should always be research evidence in my view. Having spent the last ten years as a trainer and consultant, advocating an evidence-based approach to school improvement, it seems logical to recommend that school leaders share the rationale behind their decisions about how they are aiming to achieve better outcomes for their pupils. This has become increasingly common in the English primary school system, especially in documents like the Pupil Premium strategy, so that stakeholders such as parents, local authority and trust officers, governors and Ofsted inspectors can readily see the reasons why certain actions and approaches have been adopted. The terms parental involvement and parental engagement are both widely used in the literature, with a variety of definitions apparent for both. I will return to the distinctions between the terms used, as well as considering which it might be advisable to adopt in practice, later in the book.

As you read the following account of the key research, you will probably notice that I have largely presented my findings in chronological order. The one exception is the work of Hoover-Dempsey and Sandler, who were carrying out research in the nineteen nineties, as was Epstein, whose framework I discuss in the preceding section. She also originally published her research in the subject of 'parent engagement' in the nineties, focusing on the *how* of the matter, but continues to work in this field of education to this day. Hoover-Dempsey and Sandler came up with a model that focused instead on the *why* of 'parental involvement', so their two pieces were seen by some as complementary. This is why I have put them together in this account of the research narrative.

A literature review by Desforges and Abouchaar (2003)

My own entry point when researching the area of parent engagement was a study commissioned by the then DfES (Department for Education and Skills) in 2003, carried out by Professor Charles Desforges with Alberto Abouchaar. Entitled *The Impact of Parental Involvement, Parental Support and Family Education on Pupil Achievements and Adjustment: A Literature Review*. The report looked at the English language research available into the relationship between parental involvement and support, as well as family learning, on pupil outcomes and their adjustment to what the school system offered (Desforges and Abouchaar 2003). A number of consistent findings emerged:

- Parental involvement is strongly positively influenced by the child's level of attainment: the higher the level of attainment, the more parents get involved.
- Parental involvement in the form of 'at-home good parenting' has a significant positive effect on children's achievement and adjustment.
- Differences between parents in their level of involvement are associated with social class, poverty, health and also parental perception of their role and their levels of confidence in fulfilling it.
- Some parents are put off by feeling put down by schools and teachers.

One key conclusion was that parents indirectly influence their child's educational outcomes through shaping their self-concept as a learner and setting high aspirations. The authors proposed a model to explain what they felt was happening when parent engagement was at its best, which we'll return to in the next chapter.

I was intrigued by the first bullet point in the previous section, which went hand in hand with the observation from some studies that greater parental involvement with school appeared to reduce pupils' outcomes. There were inconsistencies it seems as to the definition of parental involvement being used by researchers, including such terms as 'good parenting' and 'talking to teachers', and it's clear that cause and effect are not always obvious from simplistic data. For example, when a child is not coping well with their learning it may often be the case that parents will have more reason to come into school, but this doesn't mean that the visits are responsible for the negative impact on the pupil's educational success. There is a tendency to use attendance at school events such as parents' evenings as a proxy measure for parental involvement, but this research finding appears to call that approach into question.

Desforges and Abouchaar reproduced an adapted diagram from one particular study (Nechyba et al. 1999), which outlined the possible influences on a child's outcomes, and it can be found in Figure 1.1. This highlights the varied forces on a child's learning, indirectly through their developing characteristics, which may change considerably during the primary school years, especially perhaps during Years 5 and 6. Parental involvement at home and school are just two of a number of interrelated factors, but both appear from the research to be important predictors of educational success.

Another finding suggested that the most significant factor was 'home discussion'. Regardless of the family's economic circumstances, the more the children conversed with their parents in the home, the better they learned at school. However, in the sample used for this piece of research it wasn't clear that the schools concerned were able to have much influence on the amount of discussion taking place.

One study, quoted on p. 26 of Desforges and Abouchaar, replicated another piece of research, looked at longitudinal data from the USA and suggested that parental activity in school had a minimal impact on a pupil's attainment. This is not to say that having parents helping in school doesn't have benefits, such as raising their own self-esteem, but a direct link with their children's learning hasn't been made in the research. The authors do suggest

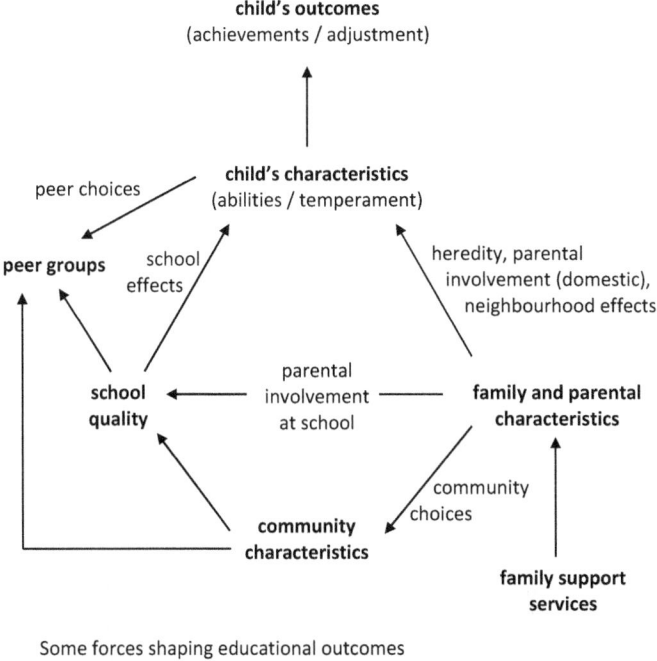

Figure 1.1 Some forces shaping educational outcomes (achievement and adjustment)

that parental in-school involvement may be a 'lubricant' for at-home involvement, as well as providing a helpful conduit for information passing in both directions in ways that might support learning. As far as can be seen, family learning activities were not what was being investigated here, so care needs to be taken when assessing the potential benefits of such schemes.

In summarising a chapter on the processes of parental involvement the authors suggested that parental influences arise in the following way:

They go on to say:

> Parental behaviours which manifest parental involvement change across the age range. With younger children, direct help with school relevant skills is appropriate and foundational. With older students, activities which promote independence and autonomy more generally become more relevant. This tentative outline model explains why parental involvement in the home is significantly more effective than parental involvement in the school. The former is more enduring, pervasive and direct. The latter is less so.
>
> (p. 35)

Another chapter in this valuable review of published research considered the effect of ethnicity on the relationship between parental involvement and pupil achievement (pp. 37-40). At that time most of the research was carried out the USA, and the crossover between ethnicity and socioeconomic status wasn't always accounted for. Important differences were identified

4 Research evidence

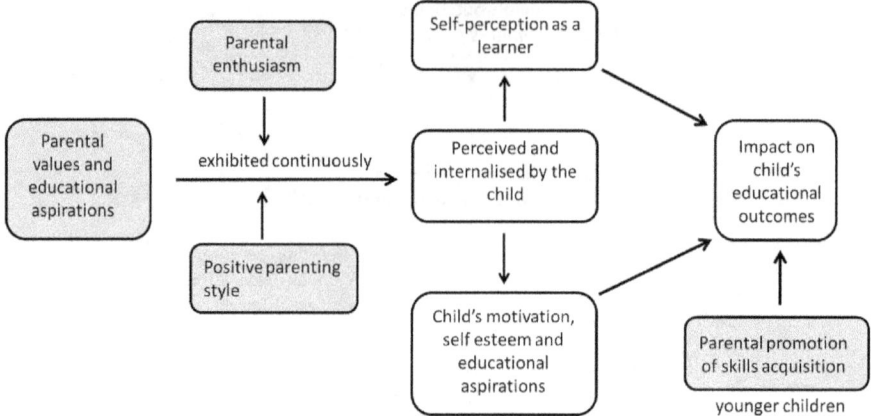

Figure 1.2 Suggested processes of parental involvement
Source: Based on *Desforges and Abouchaar (2003, p. 35)*

between ethnic groups in the ways in which they demonstrated their support and involvement, but the basic mechanisms and the level of impact on children's outcomes was consistent across all ethnic groups. Furthermore, one study of Mexican-American pupils suggested that familiarity with the English language had no obvious effect on parents' readiness to get involved in their child's learning. An important finding was that the ethnic culture of the family can be very important in determining how parental aspirations and values are modelled in the home.

There is enormous variation in the degree to which parents see it as their role to support their child's education and how confident they feel about doing so, sometimes described as 'personal efficacy'. Understandably, it appears that parental engagement tends to decrease as children get older. Other factors that appear to reduce involvement include single-parent status, maternal psychosocial difficulties and material poverty. Research evidence also suggests that many parents feel put off from becoming involved by the way some teachers treat them. Children themselves are also thought to have an influence on their parents' willingness to engage with their learning.

Two researchers (Edwards and Alldred 2000) talked to 70 children in Years Six and Nine, and discovered that the pupils could be passive or active in encouraging, or discouraging, their parents to be active or inactive in their education. Some were spontaneous about describing their school day, motivated chiefly by their parents' company, while others responded to their parents' prompts in a semi-passive way, which was more about pleasing the parents than meeting their own need to share. These interactions nearly always took place at home and were seldom about the child wanting to improve their level of achievement but rather about the intimacy that they felt in sharing their news.

On the other hand, many pupils were active in discouraging parent engagement, frequently out of a sense of protecting their parents from the embarrassment or boredom of having to listen to accounts of the school day. Also, letters about expensive trips, for example, might conveniently be lost on the way home to spare parents the stress of having to find the money to pay for them. Such efforts did not appear to imply child-parent alienation but rather a sense of increasing autonomy that comes with greater independence towards and beyond the end of Key Stage 2.

When pupils were asked why they thought their parents weren't involved in school life the answer generally didn't suggest that this was an active stance but rather because they were too busy or weren't 'the type'. Those children who didn't push for their parents to engage saw it as the adults' responsibility, if they had the resources or the inclination. Gender differences were also observed, with girls more likely than boys to encourage parent engagement, especially in the home. Social class also seemed to be a factor, with 'middle class' pupils more likely to be comfortable with the idea of parental involvement and their 'working class' counterparts more resistant to 'institutional incursions into family life', as they are described by Edwards and Aldred. The latter seemed on the whole to be more autonomous when it came to their parents' involvement in school. In summary, this research suggests that children often play a dynamic role in influencing how involved their parents are in their education, both at school and in the home.

A meta-analysis by Jeynes (2005)

In 2005 the Harvard Family Research project, which was then part of the Harvard Graduate School of Education, published a meta-analysis of research into the link between parental involvement and student achievement from kindergarten to twelfth grade, written by William H. Jeynes. The purpose was to determine 'the extent to which certain expressions of parental involvement are beneficial to children' (Jeynes 2005). He estimated the impact of parental involvement on overall educational outcomes to be between 0.5 and 0.6 standard deviations, describing the range of scores achieved by pupils whose parents were highly involved as substantially higher than for those whose parents were less involved.

Jeynes went on to break down the different aspects of parental involvement into facets such as communicating or reading with one's child (both time-consuming activities), parental style and expectations (more subtle behaviours) and more demonstrative aspects such as having household rules or attending school events, both of which were found to be less effective. Jeynes found that parental expectations had the biggest effect size of all the facets identified. His findings suggested that parental engagement programmes also affected pupil outcomes but not as much as pre-existing parental support. Results also supported the view that parental involvement was influential across all the ethnic groups studied.

The implications for practice listed by Jeynes were:

- Parental involvement makes a significant difference to educational outcomes.
- Voluntary involvement and parental engagement programmes are both effective, so schools should develop strategies that enhance and deliver them.
- School leaders, teachers and other relevant staff should be aware of the facets of parental involvement that have the greatest impact and facilitate or encourage them.

The project became independent of Harvard University in 2017 but continues in the form of the Global Family Research Project, providing resources, articles and case studies intended to inform and inspire those who access it through the website or subscription.

Epstein (2009)

A well-recognised American researcher and prolific author in the field of parent engagement is Joyce Epstein, who has worked with collaborators since the nineteen nineties to refine a framework of six types of parent involvement, sometimes called the school-family-community partnership model. Based on her observations of parental involvement that she and her collaborators felt raise pupils' outcomes, the six types that she proposed were:

1. Parenting: family practices and the home environment support children as learners, and school understands its families.
2. Communicating: teachers, pupils and parents design effective communication both ways between school and home.
3. Volunteering: teachers, pupils and parents recruit and organise parent help and support and see parents as an audience for pupil activities.
4. Learning at home: the school provides information, methods and training to enable parents to support their children effectively with homework activities and other curriculum-related tasks.
5. Decision making: the school includes parents in decisions about their children's education and develops parent leaders and representatives.
6. Collaborating with the community: partner services and community resources are integrated into the education process to strengthen the school's programmes, the family's processes and children's learning and development.

Epstein and her co-workers didn't just come up with diagrams to explain their theories but also produced a series of three tables that outline in great detail examples that they had seen of each type of parent involvement and its consequences. The first table outlines each type with a short set of examples from practice for each one, the second suggests the challenges that might need to be overcome in order to implement each type successfully, and the third gives examples of the impact of the types on parents, pupils and educators. These are readily available on the internet if you would like to explore them further. Epstein has continued to refine her ideas, with the fourth edition of her handbook for school-family-community partnerships being published in 2019. She continues to be involved in a community of research schools through Johns Hopkins University in the USA, which then provides schools and districts with guidance about evidence-based programmes that they could implement.

Hoover-Dempsey and Sandler (1997)

Also working in the nineteen nineties in the field of parental involvement, as they called it, were Kathleen Hoover-Dempsey and Howard Sandler. In 1995 they sought to explain why

Level 5   Child / student outcomes

Skills & knowledge

Personal sense of efficacy for doing well in school

Level 4   Tempering / mediating variables

| Parent's use of developmentally appropriate involvement strategies | Fit between parent's involvement strategies & school expectations |

Level 3   Mechanisms through which parental involvement influences child outcomes

| Modelling | Reinforcement | Instruction |

Level 2   Parent's choice of involvement forms, influenced by

| Specific domains of parent's skill & knowledge | Mix of demands on total parental time and energy (family, employment) | Specific invitations & demands for involvement from child & school |

Level 1   Parent's basic involvement decision, influenced by

| Parent's construction of the parental role | Parent's sense of efficacy for helping her / his children succeed in school | General invitations & demands for involvement from child & school |

Figure 1.3 Model of the parental involvement process
Source: Based on *Hoover-Dempsey and Sandler (1997, p. 4)*

parents' involvement in their children's education made a difference and, in a subsequent paper, what caused them to do so (1997). Their five-stage model, based on wider research and their own activity in the field, is intended to represent what they discovered and consists essentially of the following:

They approached the involvement process, as they called it, from the parents' perspective, trying to determine the psychology of the different stances that parents took to becoming involved in their children's education. The suggestion is that parents begin at Level 1 by choosing to become involved in their child's learning at home and in school, based on their understanding of what it means to be a parent in relation to learning, their sense of being able to deliver this aspect of the role and their subsequent receptiveness

8 Research evidence

to invitations and demands from the school and their child. This may then develop up through the other levels of involvement, with the contributing factors taken into account, culminating in Level 5, where it becomes evident that child or student outcomes are being improved.

A digest of research by Lucas (2010)

In 2010 Bill Lucas produced a very helpful digest of the research outcomes available for teachers and parents on the impact of parent engagement on the success of learners. It was part of a series called *Research into Practice*, published by the Centre for Real-World Learning at the University of Winchester, comprising a brief history of the topic, what the key research said at the time and a series of practical ideas for schools and parents who were interested in developing better learning outcomes through improved engagement. The style is engaging, and the digest is very easy to read. Lucas starts with a headline statement that 75 to 85 percent of a child's waking hours are spent outside of school. He goes on to acknowledge the importance of the quality of schools and the nature of a pupil's peer group but suggests that it is principally from home that children acquire lasting effects on their 'character, mindset and attainment'. He restates in clear and concise language what we have seen already in this chapter. Parents can help their child most by:

- having 'regular and meaningful' conversations about learning
- setting high aspirations
- demonstrating their own interest in learning (at home and at school)
- showing support for that learning

He goes on to say that, whilst there is a clear link between effective parent engagement and improved educational outcomes for pupils, it is unclear precisely why certain approaches adopted by educators and parents appear to work. The challenges laid down in the document are for global education departments to develop their understanding of this key area and for schools to adopt practices that could have a significant impact on helping their pupils to become more effective learners.

A brief history of parent engagement describes the journey in the developing world from parents being the sole educators of their children through to a situation where schools were sometimes seen as closing the school gates to parents and using parent-teacher associations simply to raise funds for the school, rather than to foster a joint approach to children's learning. Lucas recognises a move towards parenting programmes in recent decades, aimed at supporting families in socioeconomically deprived areas where parents have not felt 'able or willing' to help with their children's education. Throughout the paper, Lucas points out that learning is about much more than just academic and vocational outcomes but is also about developing a child's 'habits of mind, dispositions and wider skills', which he goes on to describe.

With regard to parental involvement in learning, he draws on the 2008 work of two American researchers, working in Minnesota, Sandra Christenson and Cathryn Peterson, whose list of constructive activities at home to support the development of effective learners includes:

the use of interesting vocabulary, discussions about school progress and external events, encouragement to read for a range of purposes and to try new things, cultural activities such as visiting libraries and museums and completing everyday household tasks. It appears that time spent with adults who share their own enthusiasm for learning new things is generally positive.

Lucas also quotes the internationally respected John Hattie (2009), whose work on the factors affecting pupil achievement continues to develop. At the time, he stated that 'parents can have a major effect in terms of the encouragement and expectations that they transmit to their children'. Hattie's most up-to-date global research suggests an effect size of 0.42 for parental involvement and 0.70 for parental expectations, although for parenting programmes the figure is lower at 0.35 (www.visiblelearningmetax.com/influences).

A number of key factors are identified as being important when parents decide whether or not to support a school in the education of their children:

- their own experience of school as a child
- how much time they have to offer given their work or other commitments (e.g. carer)
- how clearly and sincerely the school communicates a desire to engage them
- the extent to which parents see educational success as 'part of their job as a parent'.

In Chapter 2 we will look at these factors in more detail when we consider in depth the model of effective parental involvement proposed by Desforges and Abouchaar and alluded to in the factors described.

Lucas notes a number of tensions in the research findings, one of which arises from the observation that parents tend to be more involved with the school when there are problems with their child's learning, rather than when things are going well, which makes attributing cause and effect problematic. Lucas suggests that for parents the phrase 'parental engagement' might mean supporting children's learning, whereas for teachers and other school staff it might be associated more with attempts to improve children's behaviour. At the end of the digest there is a helpful series of practical ideas for schools and parents, which we will return to in later chapters, where particular characteristics will be discussed in more detail.

A review of best practice for the DfE (2011)

Janet Goodall and John Vorhaus, supported by other researchers, produced a review of global interventions that were seen as effective in supporting parental involvement. It was commissioned by the Department for Education (DfE) in 2011, in response to Desforges and Abouchaar's work, and sought to identify methods that schools could adopt with those parents who were less involved in their children's education or not involved at all. The intention was to:

- identify practices that promote parental behaviours most likely to lead to 'educational outcomes'
- identify the particular features that underpin these practices
- present a profile of 'what success looks like' for schools, services, practitioners and parents

Research evidence

The executive summary includes a very helpful summary of evidence, which pulls together the main findings for those interested in maximising parent engagement with what happens in their school or classroom. Firstly, it considers school-home links, insisting that a whole-school approach is essential, with an integrated parent-engagement strategy aimed at improving children's learning, rather than seeing such activity as a bolt-on to mainstream approaches. The need for staff training and coaching is also recognised, as is the advisability of finding out about parents' attitudes to and values about engagement in school life and learning. It also recommends that clear, specific and targeted information is provided to parents about what is on offer and what might be expected of them. The authors propose that any strategy should be outward-facing, drawing where appropriate on the views of parents as well as evidence from the wider community of schools and other services. Information Communication Technology (ICT) is flagged up as a highly effective means by which parents can keep up with their children's learning and an efficient use of their time for teachers, teaching assistants and learning mentors. Likely challenges to successful parent engagement are also outlined, including a lack of confidence or knowledge on the part of school staff, a lack of understanding about how parents are already involved in their children's learning and the logistical barriers for many parents through insufficient money, time or transport.

Secondly, the summary suggests the benefits of providing support and training for parents, with specific programmes potentially delivering recognition by parents of any problems that exist, gaining knowledge and skills in behaviour management and developing the confidence and empathy to use these skills to greater effect. It appears that equipping parents to deliver particular reading skills to their children, rather than just encouraging them to read to them, can deliver greater improvements in literacy learning. There appears to be little evidence on the wider subject-specific impacts of at-home learning support, other than some effects in numeracy. In terms of approaches that work it seems that those programmes that include some academic focus, as well as developing parenting skills, have the greatest impact on children's outcomes. As a final observation in this section the importance of a parental needs analysis is suggested. Understanding the cultural norms and expectations of different groups of parents is deemed to be essential, as is targeting specific programmes based on the insights gained. Recognising what parents are already doing to support their children's learning is also thought to be a key part of designing effective approaches intended to build on this in developing fuller engagement.

Thirdly, family and community-based interventions are addressed, describing a range of family programmes in literacy and, to a lesser extent, numeracy, with evidence pointing to improvements in both aspects of learning, as well as other areas such as motivation and broader achievement. Gains in academic outcomes, especially for disadvantaged children, have been demonstrated, often going beyond the duration of the projects. Partnership arrangements are seen as essential to a cohesive approach to parent engagement, with schools co-operating with other services such as the police, social care and health teams. At best, information is appropriately shared both ways between the different providers, including childcare settings and schools at the various points of transition for pupils. Importantly, the final paragraph in this section points out that whilst some of the evidence is robust, there are gaps, and it is not yet possible to evaluate in great detail the different approaches used, or how they might be most effectively applied at different stages of a child's development.

The summary section goes on to propose a possible structure for strategic thinking about parental engagement, potentially giving rise to a school or service strategy document. The following key features are identified in the review's findings:

- Planning – a full needs analysis, agreed mutual priorities, monitoring and evaluation of actions and approaches taken, wide awareness process to help parents and school staff buy into plans.
- Leadership – essential to the success of a strategy, often by a senior leader, and potentially including shared central leadership of a wider programme in a group of schools.
- Collaboration and engagement – proactive instead of reactive, sensitive to individual families' circumstances, recognising parents' ability to contribute, empowering.
- Sustained improvement – links to whole-school development or improvement planning, ongoing funding and training, community involvement at all stages, continuous evidence-based review and revision.
- Challenges – parental perceptions of school (lack of encouragement and information), parental barriers (costs, time, transport, language, literacy, numeracy, lack of confidence), sustainability (retaining committed and inspiring leaders, maintaining commitment across staff teams with multiple competing priorities, continuous access to funding and other resources), reaching and involving parents who are determined not to be involved with their children's school or learning, lack of relevant staff experience and knowledge.

The main body of the report consists of evaluations of individual pieces of research, such as that carried out in 2009 by Lindsay *et al.* into the effectiveness of parent support advisors (PSAs). A group of local authorities was involved in a pilot study, with data being collected from parents, PSAs, line managers and other professionals. More than 80 percent of the line managers interviewed felt that the PSAs had improved parents' engagement with their children's learning, almost 85 percent stated that pupil attendance had improved, over 90 percent described a better relationship between school and the parents concerned and parents were 'overwhelmingly positive about the experience, with 100% reporting that they felt they had been understood and respected. And 95% that they felt more confident to deal with emerging school-related difficulties' (p. 33).

The executive summary concludes with the following statement:

> There is now a sufficient body of information to provide a firm basis for a programme of ongoing development and research – trialling, testing, evaluating and building on the best evidence we have.
>
> (p. 11)

A guidance report from the EEF (2018)

Given that the previous sentence was written in 2011, it is disappointing that the Education Endowment Foundation (EEF) stated something very similar in its own guidance report aimed at English schools, entitled 'Working with Parents to Support Children's Learning' (2018). This suggests that the intervening years were to some extent wasted in research terms, in spite of the introduction in England, by the British government, of the Pupil Premium, aimed at closing the academic gap between disadvantaged and other pupils at all Key Stages in education.

Sir Kevan Collins, then CEO of the EEF, included this paragraph in his foreword to the report (p. 4):

> To arrive at the recommendations, we reviewed the best available international research and consulted with teachers and other experts. The evidence in this area is not yet as strong as we would like, so an over-arching recommendation focuses on the importance of planning and monitoring your school's parental engagement activities to get the most out of them. Other recommendations look at the best ways to communicate with parents, and strategies for supporting learning at home.

However, on a more encouraging note he makes this statement earlier in the same section:

> We know that levels of parental engagement are consistently associated with children's academic outcomes. We also know that a parent's job, education and income matters less to their child's development than what they actually do with them.

The EEF is a government-funded but independent charity, created in 2011 by the Sutton Trust, to advise English schools on the most effective ways to break the link between family income and educational achievement, often seen as directing school leaders towards spending their Pupil Premium Grant wisely. The report is divided into four sections, or recommendations, which will be considered briefly in turn.

Recommendation one: 'Critically review how you work with parents'. In the summary for this section the report states that in spite of the potential impact of effective parent engagement most schools don't have an explicit plan for how they work with parents and less than 10 percent of teachers have received any training on this area of their practice. Schools are advised to critically review their aims and current provision, focus on areas that have the most supportive evidence, find out from less-involved parents what support they would like and plan defined aims that they can monitor progress towards.

Recommendation two: 'Provide practical strategies to support learning at home'. For younger children, encouraging shared book reading is suggested as a central component of parent engagement, as is playing with letters and numbers (digits). Conversations about learning, especially those connected with book reading, are also identified. Schools are advised to help parents to create a regular routine, encouraging their children to have good homework habits and to self-regulated learning by setting goals, planning and managing their time, rather than providing direct support for homework tasks. Fostering summer reading is described as a promising approach, although not currently a common one in schools.

Recommendation three: 'Tailor school communications to encourage positive dialogue about learning'. There appears to be a link between well-designed school communications and outcomes such as attainment and attendance, at relatively low cost. This relationship is thought to be strengthened when messages are personalised and linked to positive messages wherever possible, such as those that celebrate pupil achievement. Data suggests that only half of parents consider that they have been consulted about how they could be involved in supporting their child's learning, so there is also a recommendation that effective two-way communication should be developed. Those parents who have less direct contact with school, such as those of older children, will rely even more on effective messaging.

Recommendation four: 'Offer more sustained and intensive support where needed'. In this section's summary the report suggests that schools should identify families' specific needs in relation to engagement, asking them where possible what they would like to enable them to support their children's learning more effectively. It is recognised that targeting of resources might be needed but suggests that this needs to be done sensitively to avoid stigmatising parents and to encourage participation. Parents should be encouraged to believe that they are partners with the school, with a focus on improving their sense of efficacy in this. Where group activities to develop parental support of learning are provided, schools are advised to use face-to-face recruitment, to find convenient times and places for them to happen and to deliver them in an informal and welcoming environment, all of which are thought to be important factors in maximising attendance.

The report contains very detailed advice in every section, with the supporting evidence referenced throughout. A series of case studies is included, some of which introduce specific programmes that the EEF has evaluated as part of its research remit.

Drawing on research to suggest how more parents might become engaged with learning (Goodall 2017)

In her book, *Narrowing the Achievement Gap: Parental Engagement with Children's Learning*, published in 2017, Janet Goodall draws on the available international evidence and her own considerable experience as a researcher and programme facilitator in the field of parental engagement to propose some key ways in which parental engagement in learning, as opposed to the more limited parental involvement in schooling, can be helpful in closing the 'achievement gap' observed especially in the English school system. She provides evidence to suggest that advantaged children are more likely to have the social and cultural capital to succeed in the current educational system, largely because their parents are able to pass on to them the aspiration, skills and attitudes necessary to do so. By contrast for many disadvantaged parents the system is much more difficult for them to support their children through, even where their desire to be effective is strong.

She recognises the widespread use of the Epstein and Hoover-Dempsey frameworks but suggests that both of them focus more on how successfully parents are engaging with school staff, rather than the degree to which they are doing so with their children's learning, especially in the home. Given that the latter factor is what research suggests is most likely to lead to improved outcomes Goodall proposes a straightforward model to outline the changes that she believes schools could make to improve their own practice, whilst also advocating in her book a number of far-reaching system changes that would radically transform society's view of the place that schooling has in a wider understanding of how learning can be developed in children, young people, families, communities and staff in school, as well as challenging the current understanding of who is responsible for providing successful education.

The implication of the model is that as the relationship between parents and the school moves down through the continuum's three broad descriptors, with brief examples, as schools and parents develop their own understanding of what a genuine partnership approach, rather than a school-centric one, can become. Goodall points out that all parents are different, with cultural factors impacting on the ways in which care and support for learning are displayed, and she suggests that power in the relationship between school staff and parents often lies

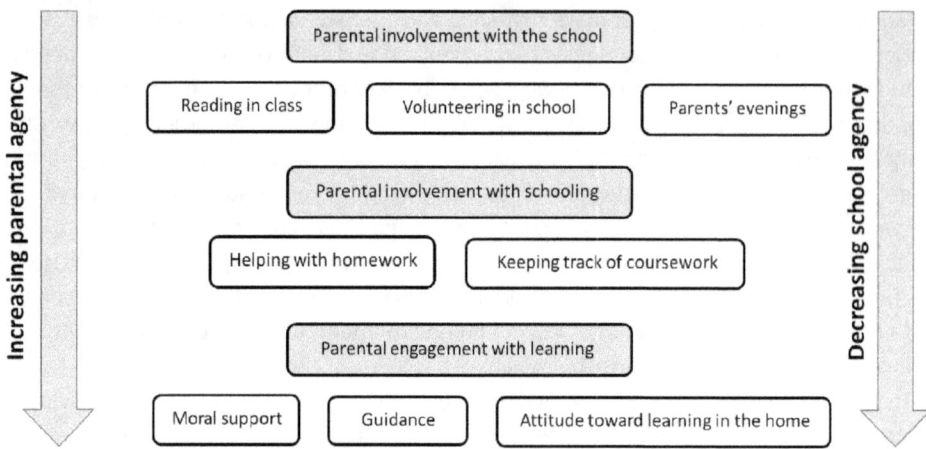

Figure 1.4 Parental engagement continuum
Source: Based on *Goodall (2017, p.93)*

with the former, a view supported in England by the 2015 Ofsted framework in place as she wrote, which stated that 'school staff should tell parents how to support their children, inform them of issues and provide guidance for parents' (p.90).

Goodall makes the following claims about a partnership approach to parental engagement, where teachers and support staff see themselves as 'experts' in schooling (imparting skills, knowledge and attitudes in an institutional context) but see parents as 'experts' in many aspects of their own child's learning and development, evident outside the school, but often not known or recognised by those who work in it:

> This new understanding of the place of schooling allows us to finally make sense of, and to integrate, one of the most important findings from the research literature; schools cannot directly affect what goes on in the home, yet this is where change needs to take place. Partnership working removes the need for schools to change what goes on in the home – this is the sphere of parents and families – but rather allows staff, as schooling professionals, to support parents more effectively as they engage with their children's learning.
> (p.90)

She suggests that using the term 'hard-to-reach parents' can be unhelpful, as it might be more useful at times to ask the question, 'Is it parents or perhaps schools which are hard to reach?' She cites the work of Myers and Myers (2015), who found that 'nearly all parents want to be involved in the educational lives of their children'. Goodall adds: 'even if they lack the resources to do so, as the system now stands' (p.101). Furthermore, she contends that school communication with parents is frequently seen as being at the heart of successful engagement with children's learning, whereas research indicates that the key is actually 'the relationship between parent and child and the atmosphere this creates around learning in the home' (p.101).

Social and cultural capital are highlighted as key factors in parents' ability to support their children's learning, based on their own feelings of self-efficacy and self-belief, and their children's familiarity with such capital. Goodall quotes Rodríguez-Brown (2009), who points out that schools 'tend to favour middle-class cultural ways and values' and this 'seems to hurt the opportunity for success of children whose language and culture are different from what is expected in school settings'.

Goodall goes on to suggest that change within individual schools will only happen if school leaders are convinced about the possibilities of effective parental engagement in learning. She advocates attention being given specifically to this crucial aspect of education in the teaching and learning policy, as well as other appropriate documents. On page 124 the following recommendations for schools appear: 'be systematic; embed engagement; be creative; move from giving information to communicating; evaluate interventions; work with others; [address] school readiness and transition'. She also provides a number of practical examples which can be found in the appendix of this book, although it is advisable to look carefully at the match of contexts when attempting to adopt, and possibly adapt, ideas from others.

Whilst working at the University of Bath, Goodall helped to produce a toolkit to support schools in their efforts to audit and improve their work in relation to parental engagement which, at the time of writing, can be readily accessed online.

Equipping parents to support their child's learning (Hattie and Hattie 2022)

In his latest book, written with his son Kyle (a primary school teacher) and published in 2022, *10 Steps to Develop Great Learners: Visible Learning for Parents*, John Hattie suggests ten mind frames for parents who would like to make their own contribution to their child's learning, alongside the efforts of their teachers. The ten mind frames, with brief summary, are:

1	I have appropriately high expectations.	The Goldilocks principle – not too hard, not too easy plus not too boring.
2	I make reasonable demands, and I am highly responsive to my child.	A reasoning and listening approach to parenting develops autonomy, interpersonal skills and autonomy.
3	I am not alone.	A child's worldview is enhanced through knowing and relating to other people.
4	I develop my child's skill, will and sense of thrill.	The combination of skills, disposition and motivation.
5	I love learning.	It is important to help a child to look for the learning zone ahead of them – the next best challenge.
6	I know the power of feedback and that success thrives on errors.	How a child receives the feedback they are offered makes all the difference to its impact.
7	I am a parent, not a teacher.	Promoting at home the language of learning should help a child to succeed at school.
8	I expose my child to language, language, language.	Exposing a child to talking, listening, reasoning and explaining and encouraging them to join in with all three.
9	I appreciate that my child is not perfect nor am I.	A child needs to develop the skills to evaluate situations and people and to mitigate risk if necessary.
10	I am an evaluator of my impact.	Parents know more than they think they do, and there is no one right way, but it helps to check that there is a positive impact on a child's learning along the way.

16 *Research evidence*

This book strikes me as a valuable addition to the literature study that has constituted this chapter, in that it provides parents with some clear suggestions as to how they can best play their part as partners with the school. I can also imagine ways in which skilled school staff might interpret the information in this book, for understanding and adoption by the widest possible set of parents in their school.

Key ideas in this chapter

- Parents' engagement with, or involvement in, their child's learning is likely to improve educational outcomes.
- What happens at home, in activities such as conversations about learning, is thought to have more impact on learning outcomes than what happens between parents and school staff in school, although the latter may encourage the former.
- There appears to be a clear link between parental and pupil aspirations about learning and the quality of outcomes.
- A number of models have been produced by researchers in the last 25 years to attempt to explain why and how parents become involved or engaged, based on the available evidence.
- Although some research has been done in this area there is seldom sufficient evidence about specific actions or approaches to be clear about their likely effectiveness.
- Cultural and economic factors affecting parental involvement and engagement are often not fully understood or taken into account by school staff.
- Two-way communication between school staff and parents is highly desirable.
- Parental engagement in learning, rather than involvement in schooling, is thought to be more beneficial to pupils.

This is not a definitive list, so you might like to add your own key ideas here from your reading so far:

Conversation starters

Here are some questions for you to consider, either on your own or with other members of the school community (e.g. staff, governors, parents, pupils).

- Which term is preferable – parental involvement or parental engagement – and why?
- What national or international evidence in support of parental involvement or engagement is the most compelling, given our school setting?

- Do we have any in-school evidence to justify the ways in which we seek to involve or engage parents in schooling or learning?
- Recognising that all parents are unique, what characterises any identifiable groups amongst the parents and carers of pupils at our school?
- To what extent should initial teacher and learning support staff training, as well as CPD, include specific content aimed at fostering effective parental partnership in children's learning?

Chapter 1 reference list

Desforges, C. and Abouchaar, A. (2003) *The Impact of Parental Involvement, Parental Support and Family Education on Pupil Achievements and Adjustment: A Literature Review*. London: DfES.

Education Endowment Foundation (2018) *Working with Parents to Support Children's Learning: Guidance Report*. London: EEF.

Edwards, R. and Alldred, P. (2000) A Typology of Parental Involvement in Education Centring on Children and Young People: Negotiating Familialisation, Institutionalisation and Individualisation. *British Journal of Sociology of Education*, 21: 435–455.

Epstein, J. L. et al. (2009) *School, Family, and Community Partnerships: Your Handbook for Action*. Third edition. Thousand Oaks, CA: Corwin Press.

Goodall, J. (2017) *Narrowing the Achievement Gap: Parental Engagement with Children's Learning*. London: Routledge.

Goodhall, J. and Vorhaus, J. (2011) *Review of Best Practice in Parental Engagement*. London: DfE/Institute of Education.

Hattie, J. (2009) *Visible Learning: A Synthesis of over 800 Meta-analyses Relating to Achievement*. London: Routledge

Hattie, J. and Hattie, K. (2022) *10 Steps to Develop Great Learners: Visible Learning for Parents*. Abingdon and New York: Routledge.

Hoover-Dempsey, K. V. and Sandler, H. M. (1997) Why Do Parents Become Involved in Their Children's Education? *Review of Educational Research*, 67 (1): 3–42

Jeynes, W. H. (2005) *Parental Involvement and Student Achievement: A Meta-Analysis*. Boston: Harvard Family Research Project

Lindsay, G., Davis, H. et al. (2009) *Parent Support Advisor Pilot Evaluation Final Report*. London: DCSF.

Lucas, B. (2010) *The Impact of Parent Engagement on Learner Success: A Digest of Research for Teachers and Parents*. Winchester: University of Winchester, Centre for Real-World Learning.

Myers, S. M. and Myers, C. B. (2015) Family Structure and School-based Parental Involvement: A Family Resource Perspective. *Journal of Family and Economic Issues*, 36 (1): 114–131

Nechyba, T., McEwan, and Older-Aguila, D. (1999) *The Impact of Family and Community Resources on Student Outcomes: An Assessment of the International Literature with Implications for New Zealand*. Wellington: Ministry of Education.

Rodríguez-Brown, F. V. (2009) *The Home – School Connection: Lessons Learned in a Culturally and Linguistically Diverse Community*. New York: Routledge.

2 A suggested model for parental engagement

Unpacking Desforges and Abouchaar's model, with suggestions as to how it might inform a primary school's strategic thinking

From the moment that I became a trainee primary teacher through my years in the classroom, then as a school leader, and finally into my current career as an educational trainer and consultant I have been convinced of the need to treat parents and carers as genuine partners in their child's education, if they are to become successful learners. As I was researching academic material to support my writing of this book one model resonated with my experiences at all levels of primary schooling, and I'm going to devote this chapter to sharing it with you. It was created by Desforges and Abouchaar (2003) to explain what had encountered in their own literature review, and I found myself wishing that I had been aware of it much earlier when I was trying to encourage parent partnership in my own practice. You can find it on page 50 of their report.

Although the title used by Desforges and Abouchaar suggests that the model is of effective parental involvement in schooling, rather than the broader area of a child's learning that Goodall described (see Chapter 1), I think the child-focused parts of the model recognise that a lot is happening outside of school too. I have made some minor additions from my own reading and experience which I will explain as I attempt to unpack the model a section at a time. You will see that I have split the model into its constituent parts, rather than confronting you initially with the whole diagram, in the hope that you will make sense more easily for yourself of the assembled model and its various propositions. There will be four versions of the model, building up these ideas, entitled Figures 2.1, 2.4, 2.5 and 2.6.

Parental capacity for involvement and school as active and reactive agent

Starting at the top of the model as published by Desforges and Abouchaar I was struck by the implication that parents' willingness and ability to become involved in their child's learning and schooling couldn't be taken for granted, whereas schools are inherently ready and prepared to engage with parents as partners in a child's education. For that reason I have added two extra factors in Figure 2.1 (not included in the original model), similar to those proposed for parents, which I believe take account of the fact that schools are not equally well-versed in, or even committed to, encouraging parents to participate as partners in their children's learning.

A suggested model for parental engagement 19

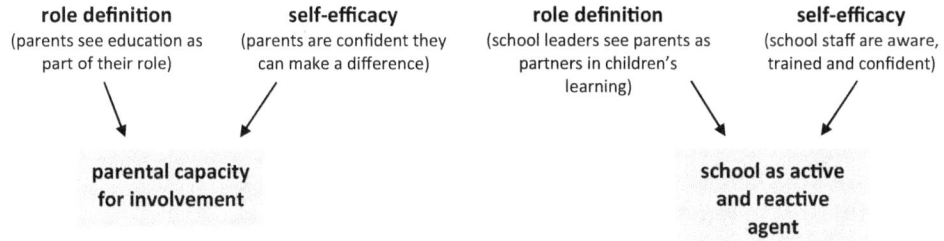

Figure 2.1 A research-based model of effective parental involvement in education: Part 1 – Foundations

It seems logical to see parental capacity for involvement as being composed of two major elements – how they define the role of parent and how positive they feel about being able to deliver support for, and encouragement of, learning. Here are some helpful definitions of key terms that are used throughout this book. The online Cambridge Dictionary has the following:

Learning – the process of getting an understanding of something by studying it
   or by experience.
Education – the process of teaching or learning, especially in a school or college,
   or the knowledge that you get from this.
Schooling – education at school.

It seems clear from these definitions that learning is something that happens from the time that a baby takes its first breath; that education is a more formal process which delivers the knowledge, skills and attitudes recognised by society as beneficial to the individual and the community, whether academic, vocational or technical; and that schooling is one part of this accumulation of learning. In Figure 2.2 I have tried to show the relationship between the concepts that will hopefully make sense to education professionals and could perhaps be shared with all of a school's stakeholders, especially parents, in order to encourage them to see the value of the wider, universal learning that they inevitably help to deliver.

Parents may rightly see themselves as their child's first teacher, having passed on knowledge and skills in their formative years, and they might relish the opportunity to continue in that role as their child moves through the school system, admittedly with less influence on school-based learning as time goes by. However, since children spend about six hours a day over approximately 40 weeks of the year in school, there is clearly a lot of other time in the year when learning of a different kind is going on. It makes sense to me that how that learning happens is as important as its content, and the way that parents and others influence that learning will have an impact on how children approach what goes on in their lessons. An often-quoted Burmese saying suggests that 'Parents are the first teachers of the children', the implication perhaps being that this isn't a sequential or chronological concept – with teachers taking over when a child reaches nursery or school age – but a collaborative one, in which the balance of the influences on a child's learning gradually shifts during their lifetime. Those of us who are parents may recognise lifelong learning in our offspring and be surprised

20 *A suggested model for parental engagement*

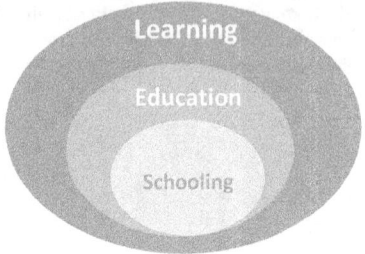

Figure 2.2 The place of schooling in a wider context

at times by the ways in which they demonstrate knowledge, interests and skills that they have picked up from us throughout their lives.

I remember as a class teacher hearing comments from parents such as 'You do maths very differently to how we did it when I was at school', and I could imagine many difficult conversations about homework activities between parents and children, principally because I was also having them with my own children at the time.

I also remember enjoying my primary school years because I seemed to be pretty successful at what was required, but for many parents school was not a happy place and success didn't come easily, if at all. Therefore, it's entirely understandable that they would approach even the simplest school-generated, home-learning tasks with trepidation, or even genuine anxiety. However, passing on life skills such as cooking, shopping, riding a bike, gardening, swimming and making good relationships may well be approached much more confidently, generating the sense of accomplishment that success brings to both parent and child.

Key elements of learning such as metacognition and self-regulation are fostered by all sorts of activities, whether they take place in a school, a home or out in the community. Research published by the Education Endowment Foundation suggests that developing these aptitudes can have a greater impact on a pupil's academic outcomes, a notional seven months' extra progress in a year, than other actions and approaches that are available.

During the pandemic many parents were called on to deliver home learning, either in place of, or support of, teachers and learning support staff in school. Even though this proved difficult for many, either through having to work from home themselves, paid or unpaid, or not feeling that they had the knowledge and skills to do so, there emerged a new understanding about what the learning process is like in practice for children. All over Britain and of course in many other parts of the world parental involvement in children's learning reached unprecedented heights, resulting for a very small but important minority in the decision to home-school on a more permanent basis.

According to DfE data, reported on the BBC News website, 'more than 40,000 pupils were formally taken out of school in the UK between September 2020 and April 2021, compared with an average of 23,000 over the previous two years', an increase of around 75 percent. However, this is in the context of 10.3 million pupils attending school in the UK, including state and independent schools, so the proportion home-schooling remains extremely small at 0.39 percent (Hattenstone and Lawrie 2021).

A suggested model for parental engagement 21

Who's responsible for a child's learning?

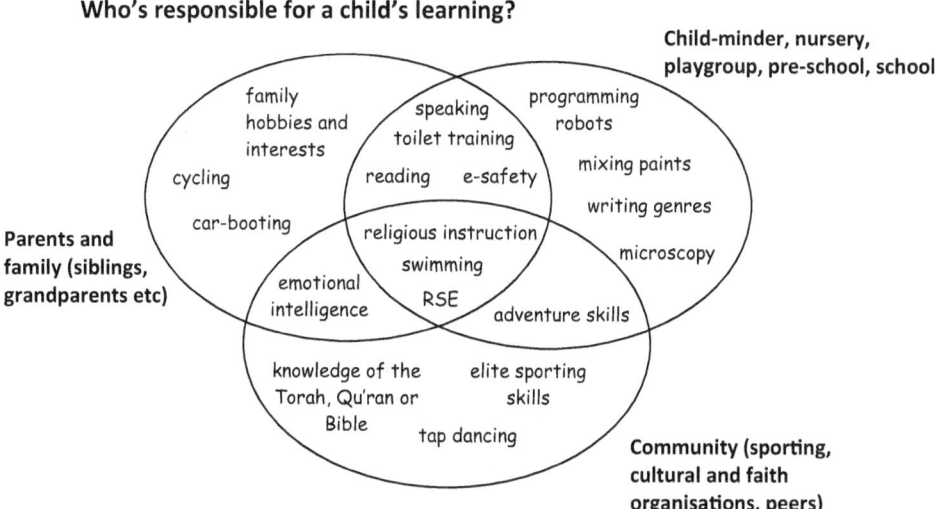

Figure 2.3 Who's responsible for a child's learning

I've devised a rather simplistic Venn diagram to explore which of three groups is responsible for delivering different aspects of learning to children – family, formal education settings and the community – which you might like to use with a cross-section of your parents, perhaps publishing your results to stimulate further discussion. I've added some general and specific areas of learning to the diagram to demonstrate how it might be used, but I'm sure that there would be some debate in a parents' workshop if you were to try to definitively place sticky notes on a large version. You will see from my worked example that I have a particular context in mind but, depending on a family's particular circumstances and expectations, the diagram might be very different.

The second aspect of this part of the model is the degree to which the school sees itself as an active and reactive agent in its relationship with its parents, not just as 'customers' or 'clients' but as partners in delivering successful learning. As with parents, it seems important that school staff at all levels are clear about those aspects of their roles that are concerned with fostering effective parental engagement. I suggest that it is only when everyone sees this as part of their job that the school will truly be able to say that it's making the best effort it can to fully engage the greatest possible number of parents in their children's learning.

Of course this isn't always easy, as leaders, teachers, learning support staff and other school staff have a huge number of calls on their time and parental engagement can be seen as yet another demand put upon them by a society that expects the school system to solve all of its problems. After more than 30 years working in and with the school system in England I think the temptation not to prioritise parental involvement is to misunderstand the absolute necessity of seeing learning, education and schooling, all three, as a joint endeavour between all those involved in a child's life. There is an unattributed African proverb that I first encountered in my FAST (Families and Schools Together) training, and which I shared with the school and community teams that I trained when delivering that programme for three years which states that 'It takes a village to raise a child'. In my mind the school is just one, albeit potentially crucial, part of that 'village'.

I have encountered school leaders who have taken a different approach, seeing parents as an inconvenient problem to be negotiated, a set of stakeholders who should be appeased where necessary and kept at arms' length as much as possible. They appear to see schooling as the purest form of learning which can only be effectively if delivered separately from the erroneous or irrelevant efforts of the parents they serve, whether those parents appear pushy, disinterested, avoidant or even harmful. I may have overstated that increasingly unusual position slightly, and it may be well-founded in a relatively small proportion of school-family encounters, but I would always want to advocate a positive approach to parents as partners, wherever they stand on the continuum of being able to deliver on that expectation and not just on the school's terms.

How seriously do we take the parents' views of their own child's nature, abilities and outlook on entry and during their time with us? As teachers, do we ask parents honestly questions like 'As one of your child's first teachers, what do I most need to know about them if they're going to learn well in my classroom?' We don't necessarily have to agree with their view, especially as our own knowledge of the child develops, but it seems to me to be respectful in the first place to ask it and to listen openly to the answer, not just during the insightful visits that early years practitioners usually make to parents in their home before a child joins the school but at the start of each school year, possibly in the autumn parents' evening or even better perhaps, during a telephone conversation at the start of September.

Safeguarding responsibilities are an essential part of the role of every member of a school's staff, and it's important that we recognise that some parents, for whatever reason, do not want the best for their child and are in reality not good for their growth, development and learning. Where this is the case schools should have the systems and processes available to act appropriately, with partner agency support where necessary. We will explore later in more detail the approaches that schools might take to help parents improve their own knowledge, skills and attitudes as they relate to their parenting, including their ability and confidence as supporters of learning.

Assuming that a school's leaders see parents as partners in their child's learning we then come to the degree to which all relevant staff subscribe to this view, are competent (and feel confident) to deliver those parts of their role that encourage and develop parental engagement, are able to monitor their success and finally, modify their approach when needed. As with most aspects of practice high-quality training will be at the heart of this key element in the model I'm proposing, although the research suggests that professional development in this area is seldom a significant part of initial teacher and learning support or childcare training. Furthermore, in-service training is only recently becoming more widely available as the importance of parental engagement is increasingly understood.

I have already referred in Chapter 1 to the work of Janet Goodall, whose own research in 2007 showed that most school staff perceived parental engagement as being about support for the school and its policies in areas like behaviour, homework or uniform. She also cited earlier research by Adelman carried out in 1992, which suggested that many programmes aimed at developing parental engagement are actually targeted at improving what goes on in school rather than children's learning at home. My own experiences of the programme mentioned earlier, Families and Schools Together, both as a school leader and a trainer, proved that it is possible to influence the dynamics of family life, parents' perceptions of the school as a partner in the child's learning and the ability of key staff to nurture and develop parental engagement in terms of the environment for learning at home. We will look more closely at FAST later in the book.

As this aspect of the model suggests, the school can be both active and reactive in its agency with regard to parental engagement. This involves approaching parents through effective communication, as well as being receptive of parents' own approaches to the school from their own perspective, as long as these are not detrimental to the pupil's wellbeing or that of staff. I have worked in the last few years with the Leading Parent Partnership Award programme (LPPA) as a trainer, supporter and verifier, and I have experienced first-hand some excellent practice where schools have carried out audits of what parents can offer the school in support of their own children's learning and that of others. Having a 'we-asked-you-said-we-did' display board in the main entrance is another excellent way of showing parents that their suggestions are taken seriously by the school. As I have already reported from the research, involving parents in improving the day-to-day running of the school, as well as direct educational input such as offering to share their knowledge and skills with pupils, setting up and supporting educational visits to workplaces or sporting venues, participating in family learning workshops and so on, are not likely in themselves to improve educational outcomes but should facilitate the development of an idea that partnership matters if children are to flourish.

Another reactive function of the school is to respond when parental engagement or involvement are not as it would want them to be. This is an area that requires sensitive but aspirational endeavour on the part of staff at all levels of responsibility, and the following chapters will contain a variety of examples from primary schools in England where this has been achieved to some extent. There are also organisations that can support schools' work in this area, more of which later in the book.

Strategic pointers

The following actions might be helpful to school leaders and practitioners in auditing and then developing practice in these first two parts of the model:

- use a variety of methods, including written, oral and digital, to carry out an audit of parents' interests, skills and connections to community organisations (making clear the school's commitment to safeguarding, of course);
- find out what training, if any, your staff have had on what successful parental involvement and engagement consist of, and how they might foster and develop them in parents of the children they work with;
- provide training that addresses gaps in staff knowledge, attitudes and skills;
- work with parents, staff, partners and community groups to develop an understanding of how children in your school learn, and share this with as many stakeholders as possible to encourage and develop this collaboration;

- offer, or signpost parents to, training that will help them to develop their literacy, numeracy and parenting knowledge, attitudes and skills so that they increase their capacity to be involved in their children's learning;
- research the organisations and resources available to develop your school's parental involvement, including the University of Bath Engaging Parents Toolkit (2019) and the Parent Engagement Network (PEN).

Parent-and-child interaction and the pupil's education self-schema

This side of the proposed model concerns the child's interaction with their parent or parents and perhaps the wider immediate family, such as grandparents, who may play a large part in the child's care and in modelling behaviours, attitudes and aspirations.

As the diagram suggests, this will consist of general parenting as well as the more focused modelling connected with education and schooling, as defined earlier. Desforges and Abouchaar are very clear on page 51 of their report about the importance of what happens at home in relation to learning, stating the following:

> The key context for parental impact on school outputs is in the home.

They go on to outline how parents may provide their children with opportunities to develop their literacy and numeracy knowledge and skills through playing word and number games. We could add activities like shopping, visits to the library, using computer games and smart phones for educational learning, as well as tasks involving construction, small world play, jigsaw puzzles and so on. For children with special educational needs some of this foundational learning will continue to be important in the home, but throughout the primary age range (and beyond into the secondary years) the main influence on school outcomes appears to be through the modelling of 'values and expectations' as the authors describe them. The passage that describes the process involved is very succinct and one that I recognise from my own teaching and leadership career as being evident in families of all types, regardless of the specific aspirations at play. These may be academic or technical ambitions, depending on a child's educational performance to date, and could be evident as early as Years 5 and 6, when children and parents might begin to consider possible careers.

> Parental involvement seems to have its major impact on children through the modelling of values and expectations, through encouragement and through interest in and respect for the child-as-learner.

It appears that children gradually internalise these familial values and expectations as they build up a picture of themselves as learners, with the term 'education self-schema' being used in the model. The narrow definition of education that I've used earlier in this chapter suggests that children might see themselves as successful learners, or not, on the basis of the limited measures that are rewarded by the school system, so the term 'learning self-schema' might be a more useful one, especially when schools try to encourage all parents, regardless of their own educational experiences, to provide positive modelling in this area. There is also a danger perhaps that children will extrapolate a poor 'education self-schema'

A suggested model for parental engagement 25

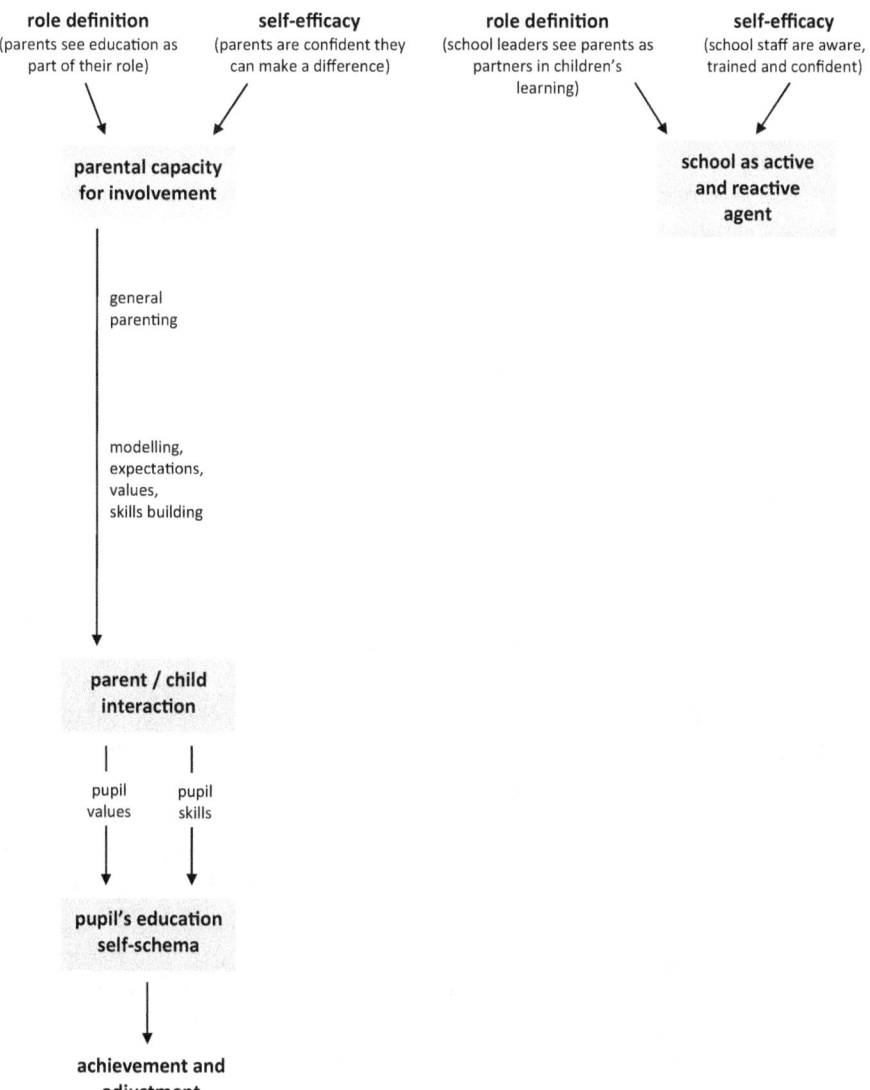

Figure 2.4 A research-based model of effective parental involvement in education: Part 1 and Part 2 – The parental contribution to learning

into their wider view of themselves as learners when they are actually highly successful learners in other less-academic domains.

The report suggests that all of the above is played out in conversations within the family about schooling and other aspects of learning and that learning itself can enhance all of these conversations in what could be described as a positive feedback loop. For the child, I suppose it's something like: 'The more I learn, the more I talk about my learning, the more I learn, especially about myself as a learner'.

This brings me almost inevitably to the subject of metacognition, a part of learning that I wish I had known much more about as a primary school practitioner and leader and an area that the EEF has long identified as a key component to maximising educational outcomes. I really only came across the term when I became a consultant and trainer, with the time to explore and grapple with such concepts. I would define it as 'understanding yourself as a learner', and it is included in an approach that I discovered as an interim leader in a co-operative trust in Barnsley in 2014. It was then that I read a book by Guy Claxton, Maryl Chambers, Graham Powell and Bill Lucas called *The Learning Powered School* (2011), an introduction to an approach that has evolved since then but which was based around 17 'learning capacities' that were organised into four learning domains (resilience, resourcefulness, reflectiveness and reciprocity). These are very practically described in an earlier book by Claxton, written with Sarah Gornall and Maryl Chambers, entitled *Building Learning Power in Action* (2005). I took what I had learned from these two publications into my work with a secondary school in Hull, and a group of primary schools in Skelmersdale, to produce a set of posters and early years songs. I have subsequently shared these with a number of schools seeking to adopt a more cohesive approach to developing their pupils' metacognition and self-regulation.

I also worked with a group of primary schools in the London Borough of Sutton during this period, at least one of which had produced a parent leaflet describing four none-gendered animal learning heroes (Tough Tortoise, Sensible Squirrel, Wise Owl and Team Ant), who were being used in early years and infant classes to foster the 'four Rs'. It became apparent that aspects of the Building Learning Power approach were eminently transferable to children's wider learning outside of school, and on reading the former of the two books referred to above I encountered a chapter devoted to 'Sending BLP home: Involving parents in their children's learning'. As well as explaining how the principles of BLP could be encouraged through home-school partnership, including a programme-specific twist on Epstein's six principles (see Chapter 1), the chapter includes other specific ideas for activities that address the questions parents might be encouraged to ask, including 'What habits am I nurturing by the way I behave with my children?' It also addresses how these will impact on their children's ability to understand themselves as learners and to develop their 'learning muscles' as BLP engagingly, if not biologically accurately, designates the different capacities.

Social learning theory (SLT) was an area of psychology that I encountered briefly during my training in, and delivery of, the FAST programme. It was developed by Albert Bandura in the nineteen sixties and seventies to explain, amongst other phenomena, how children learn from role models such as their parents. Partly because there is a cognitive mediation process between observing a behaviour and replicating it, Bandura renamed his theory social cognitive theory (SCT) in 1988. Research in this area validates the aspect of the parental engagement model that I'm unpacking here and will be probably be one of the theories underpinning parenting programmes currently in use in schools. A useful introduction to the theory, including a critical evaluation, can be found in an article on the Simply Psychology website by Saul McLeod in 2016.

Towards the end of this part of the model the arrows guide us to those parent-child interactions through which an individual pupil's education or learning self-schema emerges, out of the values and skills that they pick up in this process. This in turn contributes to their ultimate achievements, in school and beyond, as well as their ability to adjust to changing circumstances. A large part of this will be their resilience to adversity or unforeseen events, another characteristic that may have been instilled in them by the modelling experienced in their home. If we assume that a child's learning self-schema allows them to make the most of their cognitive capabilities in a specific domain, such as literacy, numeracy, technology, art or sport, then we will leave room for all children to aspire to what we might choose to call their true 'potential', an aspiration that all parents can hopefully subscribe to.

I can remember sending out questionnaires to the parents of the dockside Grimsby primary school where I was the headteacher for nearly five years, in which we included the question 'What do you see your child doing when they leave school?' It was our intention to find out what educational aspirations our parents had for their children, and all the respondents chose at least one of the following options: going to university, attending college, doing an apprenticeship and going into work. Whichever of those routes the child was to end up pursuing, a positive and healthy education or learning self-schema would seem to be a pre-requirement for the remaining school years ahead of them, especially in the secondary schools they were heading for, where greater learning independence would be necessary.

Strategic pointers

You could consider the following suggestions in response to this section of the model:

- adopt a universal programme such as the Triple P Positive Parenting Program, or review your existing provision, to enable all parents to develop their general parenting skills at whatever level they decide;
- implement a specific, coherent approach or programme to develop metacognition and self-regulation in your pupils and to support them in creating a positive and effective learning self-schema (or review what you already have in place);
- include a question (or questions) in your regular questionnaire to parents that attempts to elicit their educational aspirations for their child, within and beyond primary school perhaps;
- draw on your experiences during the COVID-19 pandemic to further develop or embed any home-learning challenges that were particularly effective in fostering parent-child interactions involving, or focussed on, their learning.

The interface between parents and school

The third version of the model includes the interface between parents and the school, a key component if an effective partnership between the two facilitators of a child's learning is to be built.

Returning to the school's active and reactive agency, the model states the importance of minimising barriers, which suggests that schools have a duty to make it as easy as possible for all parents to participate appropriately in their child's learning, both in and out of school but especially the latter. The point made earlier from the work of Janett Goodall,

28 *A suggested model for parental engagement*

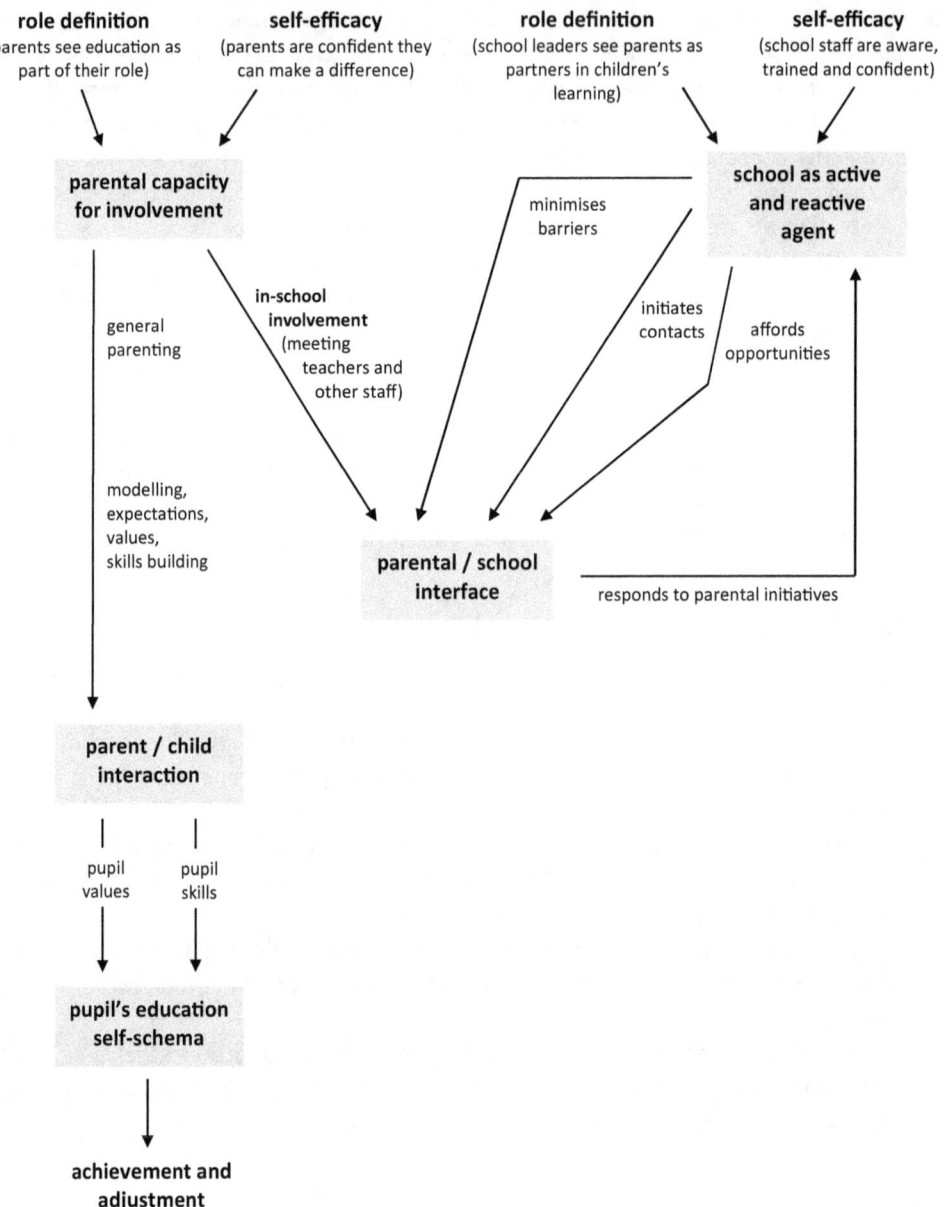

Figure 2.5 A research-based model of effective parental involvement in education: Parts 1-2 and Part 3 – The interface between parents and the school

about avoiding the term 'hard to reach' when referring to some families, is an important one, in that whilst some parents may be perceived by staff as difficult to engage with, and justifiably so, for many parents the school itself can seem equally difficult to access.

I will be referring throughout this book I'm sure to the importance of clear leadership from the top in relation to parental involvement, a factor that is well-highlighted by a piece of research undertaken by Barr and Saltmarsh (2014) in New South Wales, working with parent focus groups from a variety of catchment types in the public, Catholic and independent sectors. One of the key findings was reported in this way on page 496:

> Particularly within primary schools, parents attributed the quality of the school culture to the principal's attitude towards parent involvement in the school. A genuinely collaborative approach towards parents was seen to be fostered from the top and communicated personally by the principal.

As a primary headteacher in two very different schools in the Grimsby area I made a point of being at the gate at the beginning and end of the day and encouraged other staff to join or stand in for me when appropriate, as this seemed to me to be one of the key ways to begin breaking down any long- or short-term barriers that might exist between the school and individual parents. This is something that I had been encouraged to do as a deputy in another Grimsby school, providing a clear message on the headteacher's behalf that parents had a direct communication route into the senior leadership of the school. In my experience in those three schools there was nearly always an opportunity on each occasion to field, and to begin dealing with, at least one concern or issue before it had the chance to escalate into something more difficult to resolve. At the time I also hoped that on a more strategic level it was sending out a clear message to parents which this piece of research appears to confirm.

I have found in working with schools on their parent partnership that it can be highly beneficial to approach the site from outside the gates with a small group of key people, including administrative staff and representative parents, and to try to experience from the point of view of a new or anxious parent the signage, the entrance, the reception area, any rooms that are frequently used for meetings between staff or visitors and parents and so on. I have seen some genuine moments of realisation on those occasions for those concerned, and a real determination to make sometimes relatively simple changes to the layout of furniture, the information presented and how this is done. A more costly exercise has been tackled by many schools in trying to move safely away from the small, draughty reception area with a sliding glass hatch and nowhere to sit whilst waiting that was so common in the past. During the last ten years I have experienced some genuinely welcoming spaces, accompanied by equally positive and welcoming interactions with reception staff, not only for myself but often for the parents behind whom I've been waiting.

In the modern age, of course, another key portal for the school, especially for parents whose lives and work patterns prevent them from visiting the building easily, will be the school website. Again, I have seen very informative workshops where teams in school have approached the website as though for the first time, and from a parents' perspective. This almost always works best when parents are involved directly in pressing keys and moving cursors, while school staff observe and ask questions. Practising with a smart phone as well as a laptop or computer is also valuable, as access to key information can be problematic. You might also like to try ringing the school from outside the telephone system to see how annoying, or perhaps uplifting, the holding music is for anyone waiting to speak to someone.

Where appropriate arranging meetings outside of school, including in the parents' home, can also be safely negotiated when there is a genuine commitment to removing perceived barriers. Of course, there will be times when mistrust and antipathy on the part of parents cannot be overcome and where staff safety or safeguarding considerations are paramount, but hopefully these can be minimised with some careful but determined action on the part of leaders and school team members at all levels.

The model goes on to suggest that an effective school initiates contacts with parents and affords opportunities for meaningful interaction. Communication was a strong theme in much of the research reported in Chapter 1, and the importance of its being two-way has been pointed out by the EEF in Section 3 of their guidance document. Consulting with parents about how they might be involved in supporting their child's learning is still surprisingly rare, and not all schools have yet established messaging systems (whether digital or paper-based) that are sufficiently personalised, linked to learning and likely to lead to positive interactions, such as when success is celebrated. The following chapters will include case studies sharing what other primary schools have done in this area, but the organisations already suggested will almost certainly have ideas on their websites, within their networks and through full participation in their programmes.

Perhaps the most important arrow on this part of the diagram is the one that suggests that the school responds to parental initiatives. As a former headteacher I know how disconcerting it can be when a group of parents appears at your door with an issue of concern. Many school leaders have also become defensive over unhelpful relationships with parent fundraising groups, so much so that I have come across some primary schools in my career who have refused to have one, or limit its efforts to specific projects, approved by school leaders and with clearly defined boundaries. There is a need for clear terms of reference, of course, or relationships can sour, but trying where possible to embrace appropriate parent-led initiatives seems to me to be desirable, as a sense of real ownership and the likelihood of genuine partnership both seem to be increased in these circumstances.

Much more challenging is the need to set up systems where individual parental initiative is encouraged and where suggestions actually do make it through to the leadership of the school. I've known schools that I've worked in, and with, where coffee mornings draw what might be called the 'usual crowd' of parents who already have the ear of the parent support advisor or the headteacher. I have also come across suggestion boxes that remain empty for weeks on end. I have, however, found schools where a rolling programme of inviting small groups of randomly selected parents into school exists, at a time convenient to them, to meet the headteacher, other key staff and governors for a meaningful conversation about their experiences of the school's work with them and their children. During the COVID-19 pandemic I have even heard of schools arranging online meetings along these lines which is clearly something that could continue post-pandemic as a highly efficient way to allow the parents involved to take the initiative in making suggestions about their involvement in pupil learning.

Finally in this section comes the arrow that shows parents who feel they have sufficient capacity for involvement participating in in-school involvement, usually by meeting teachers *and other school staff* (my addition to the original model) in a variety of ways and for a range of purposes. For primary schools this part of the model includes informal conversations in the playground, at the classroom door, within the classroom, usually around the handing over of early years and infant children. Higher up the school, such conversations are more likely to take place at the school gate or over the phone, of course, but are nonetheless worthwhile and in some cases may be vital. These are the occasions on which it is crucial for all staff to be aware of the school's ethos in relation to parental involvement, as we will see in the remaining chapters of the book which will contain ideas about those characteristics of the school that are most likely to lead to secure, trusting and effective partnership between home and school.

In the majority of schools parents' evenings form a large proportion of the time allocated by schools for this purpose and how they are organised and handled varies enormously. I have been involved in, and encountered, a wide variety of models. In some schools, appointments are arranged at the parents' request, and I can remember teaching colleagues in the past who would congratulate themselves on having very few people to see on the evening in question, as this would mean that they could go home earlier. As a headteacher I favoured a system which allowed parents to request a convenient slot in the first instance, but that ensured everyone was allocated a time regardless of whether they had asked for one or not. I then encouraged follow-up texts and calls to arrange a telephone catch-up with any parents who hadn't been seen. The COVID-19 pandemic has forced many schools to devise creative alternatives to the traditional in-school format for parents' evening, and it will be interesting to see how many continue with a blended approach, depending on the needs and preferences of parents.

One of the opportunities that parents' evenings create is in the use that can be made of shared spaces like reception areas and halls, and many schools take this opportunity for welfare, learning support and home school liaison staff, as well as governors, to mingle with parents as they arrive to meet the teacher or leave after their appointments. Parents are often in a hurry to get home and carry on with their busy lives, but brief questionnaires could easily be completed, or conversations started that can be finished later, by arrangement. Even relatively simple activities like this can send out a clear message that partnership with parents really does matter to the school.

For children with special educational needs and disabilities there are additional opportunities for dialogue between teachers and parents, such as the three meetings per year recommended in England by the DfE's SEND code of practice. As well as these structured, formal meetings informal conversations will inevitably take place much more frequently to ensure that provision to meet the pupils' needs is well-understood and supported by the parents, and that their own ideas about what might work for their child are taken into account when appropriate.

Strategic pointers

Here are some questions that you might ask about the interface between parents and your school. They might be directed at teachers, learning support and administrative staff, parents or other stakeholders such as those working for other agencies and services.

- How welcome do you feel when you come into school, and how might this be improved?
- How do you find our communication systems? Is it easy to contact us when you need to? Do we keep you as informed as you would like? How do you think we could do better?

- What do you find helpful about parents' evenings and how could they be improved? Are there any advantages that you think you might find from us using online platforms to 'meet' with you about your child's learning for at least some of the time?
- If you have ideas about how you feel we might improve your child's learning by working more closely together do you know how you can put them forward? Have you done so in the past, and do you think the improved partnership worked better?

The informed parent and the child's participation

The final version of the model includes the concept of the 'informed parent', the child's participation in shaping parent-teacher interactions and the school's direct input into, and reaction to, the child's emerging learning self-schema.

I have modified the original model slightly by adapting the language in the 'informed parent' box to more accurately reflect primary practice. These final two parts of the diagram take account of the change in parents' understanding, and possibly their buy-in to, the schools aims, values, curriculum, assessment methods and expectations, and even the more focused idea of schooling discussed earlier in Figure 2.2. This will have arisen out of an effective parent-school interface, as the arrow in the diagram suggests, and should enable the parent to support and encourage not only wider learning, but also to model the school's expectations of the child to discuss, and encourage their support of, activities suggested by the child, and to become involved where they can in skills training.

Another arrow on the model describes the fact that as a child's education self-schema develops with age they tend to become increasingly involved in shaping parent-teacher interactions, for instance by taking the parents' evening or family learning workshop letter home with real enthusiasm and pushing their parent to attend. Alternatively, of course, a feeling of greater learner independence for some children might direct them to dissuading parents from attending school events by suggesting that there's no point in going or that they wouldn't enjoy it. By the end of their time at primary school I can remember my own children becoming increasingly embarrassed about having me around school, and I don't suppose that I'm alone in that.

The final arrow in the model suggests that schools as active and reactive agents have a direct involvement in a child's education and wider learning self-schema. This almost goes without saying but is a reminder to us that the partnership which we're aiming for still allows for great influence from those staff and volunteers who work with the children during their time, not just in lessons but also in the playground, in the dining room, on educational visits to museums and residential trips to adventure activity centres. The reactive dimension to this is perhaps less-easily achieved, and consists of the ways in which those staff analyse, often informally, how each child's self-schema is developing. This is potentially another way in which using programmes to teach and assess metacognition and self-regulation can prove very helpful if pupils' achievement and adjustment are to reach their potential.

Now that I have presented the entire research-based model, with my slight adaptations, it's time to look at a number of key characteristics of school staff behaviours that I believe facilitate parental involvement and engagement. I will do this in the next chapter.

A suggested model for parental engagement

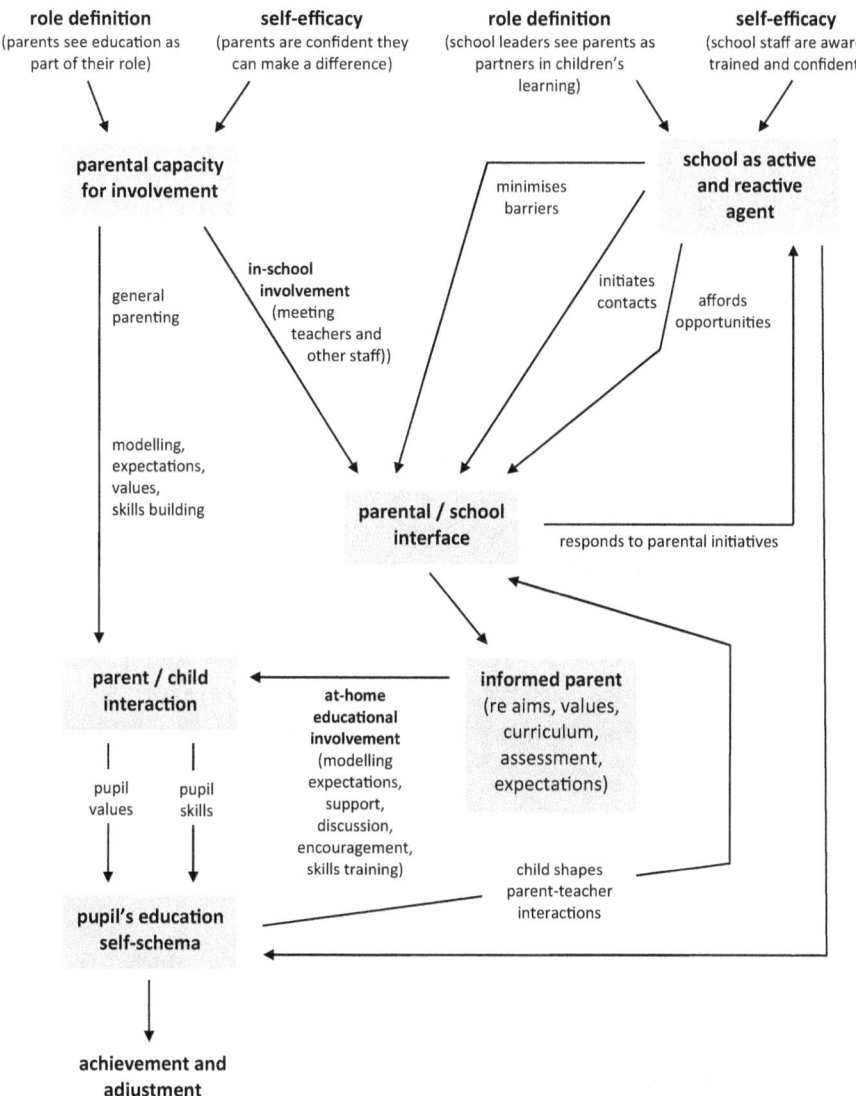

Figure 2.6 A research-based model of effective parental involvement in education: Parts 1-3 and Part 4 - The informed parent and the child's participation

Strategic pointers

The following questions might support you in analysing the extent to which your school successfully informs parents about its educational ethos, the systems it has in place to deliver learning and its expectations for parent partnership:

- How much do parents know about how our school operates and why?
- To what extent are parents able to pass this knowledge on to their children?

- How much influence do our pupils have on their parents' attendance at school events, and how much does this vary with age? How do/could we measure this?
- Do we have a way to measure the development of our pupils' learning and education self-schema? How well do they know themselves as learners?

Key ideas in this chapter

- It can be helpful for a school to adopt, adapt or create a working model for parental involvement and engagement in their child's learning.
- Parents may not recognise that one part of their role is to be their child's first teacher.
- Not all parents feel equipped to support their child's learning.
- Schools might usefully reflect on their own attitude to their parents as partners in learning and how this is communicated to parents.
- The nature of the parent-school interface is essential for developing effective parent partnership, producing at best a group of informed parents who are able to support the work of the school, and their children's broader learning, more effectively.
- As they grow, children develop an individual self-schema for learning, education and schooling which is influenced by their interactions with their parents, family, friends, the community and of course, school staff and volunteers.

This is not a definitive list, so you might like to add your own key ideas here from your reading in this chapter and any further thoughts about earlier material:

Conversation starters

Here are some broader questions for you to consider regarding the entire model outlined in this chapter, either on your own or with other members of the school community (e.g. staff, governors, parents, pupils). This not a 'tablets-of-stone' model from my point of view but rather a 'starter for ten', and you may well wish to adapt it further as I have done, without moving too far from the broad research by Desforges and Abouchaar that originally informed it.

- Which aspects of the model do I recognise from my own experiences in this and other schools?
- Which parts of the model would I like to challenge, and perhaps rewrite, to match my own views?
- Is there anything that I would want to add to the model?

Chapter 2 reference list

Barr, J. and Saltmarsh, S. (2014) "It All Comes down to the Leadership": The Role of the School Principal in Fostering Parent-school Engagement. *Educational Management Administration & Leadership 2014*, 42 (4): 491-505

Claxton, G. et al. (2011) *The Learning Powered School: Pioneering 21st Century Education*. Bristol: TLO Ltd

Desforges, C. and Abouchaar, A. (2003) *The Impact of Parental Involvement, Parental Support and Family Education on Pupil Achievements and Adjustment: A Literature Review*. London: DfES.

Families and Schools Together (FAST). Available at: www.familiesandschools.org/ (Accessed 27.2.22)

Gornall, S. et al. (2005) *Building Learning Power in Action*. Bristol: TLO Ltd

Hattenstone, A. and Lawrie, E. (2021) Covid: Home-education Numbers Rise by 75%. *BBC News*. Published 19 July 2021. Available at: www.bbc.co.uk/news/education-57255380 (Accessed 24.2.22)

Leading Parent Partnership Award (LPPA). Available at: www.awardplace.co.uk/award/lppa (Accessed 27.2.22)

McLeod, S. (2016) *Bandura – Social Learning Theory*. Available at: www.simplypsychology.org/simplypsychology.org-bandura.pdf (Accessed: 24.2.22)

Parent Engagement Network (PEN). Available at: www.penetwork.co.uk/ (Accessed 24.2.22)

Triple P Positive Parenting Program (2012). Available at: www.triplep.uk.net/uken/home/ (Accessed 24.2.22)

University of Bath (2019). *Engaging Parents Toolkit*. Available at: www.bath.ac.uk/publications/parental-engagement-toolkit/ (Accessed: 27.2.22)

3 Principles for practice in parental involvement and engagement

Suggested characteristics, behaviours and attitudes that could support successful parent partnership, when used by practitioners and parents alike

After 23 years working as a teacher and school leader in a variety of primary schools in the Grimsby and Cleethorpes area, and ten years as a trainer and consultant working alongside a wide range of school personnel, governors and parents all over England, I have come up with five characteristics and behaviours that I believe contribute to successful parental involvement and engagement. These ideas were consolidated during the pandemic in a virtual collaborative training conversation with a deputy headteacher colleague in Cornwall, whose participation on that occasion, and briefly since, galvanised my thinking. The rest of this book consists of a number of case studies intended to stimulate your own thoughts and ideas about parent partnership, organised under chapter headings from the characteristics that I'm proposing. The case studies are not meant to be exemplars since contexts are so often particular to one school or local area, but the actions and approaches they describe are offered as a potential starting point for you to adopt, adapt or leave to one side as you wish.

I'm indebted to the schools that have taken the time to share their practice with me for inclusion in this book and therefore for your consideration or inspiration. Hopefully those examples that don't appeal to you will, if nothing else, strengthen your commitment to maximising the impact of the ones that you already have in place or your determination to successfully implement any that do catch your eye, or perhaps most closely match your context.

Naturally, you will have your own ideas about the sort of ethos that fosters great parent partnership, when it's lived out by everyone in and around the school. I believe that at best the characteristics and behaviours that we exhibit as schools in our dealings with parents will be mirrored by their dealings with us and, being an optimist at heart, I would expect this scenario to be the case in the vast majority of cases. You may well have other ideas that you would want to add to those I'm putting forward, especially if the strategies that you adopt, or continue from your current practice, resonate with what you have read from the research outlined in the first two chapters.

The following diagram sets out what I think are the key elements of parent partnership, whether initiated by the school or its parents, and I will go on to expand on what I mean by them and how they have been broadly evidenced in the successful parent-school relationships that I have seen during my own teaching and leadership career or from my subsequent observations and experiences within the wider system since then.

DOI: 10.4324/9781003232070-3

Principles for practice in parental involvement and engagement 37

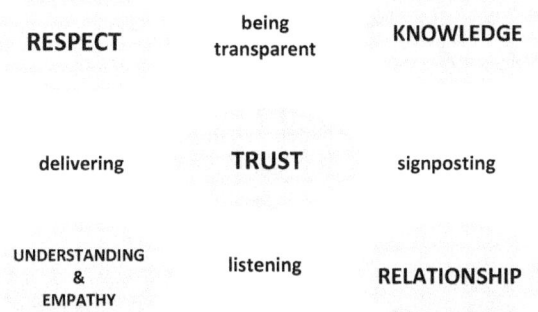

Figure 3.1 Key characteristics of effective parent partnership

I have represented the key characteristics as five nouns, with *trust* deliberately placed in the centre, as I believe that this aspect of school culture arises out of, and develops alongside, the other four. It seems to me that ideally, in each and every interaction between parent and school, the five characteristics develop mutually so that, for instance, the *respect* shown by a teacher to a child's dad during parents' evening fosters *respect* the other way. Another example might be the trouble taken by an early-years professional to acquire *knowledge* about the aptitudes of a four-year-old prospective pupil during a home visit, leading to a mum seeking further *knowledge* about how reading is taught in the reception class. Ethically, I suppose that I view the school as being responsible for initiating this two-way growth, without wanting to patronise parents in making that suggestion. I'm not naive enough to think that this will always be easy or that it will happen in every case without a great deal of effort. I also have enough experience of making repeated efforts to engage with parents, in a wide variety of educational settings, to know that in some cases, for whatever reason, it's just not possible to build a positive link.

In my recent conversations with school staff and parents, as I've sought material for the case studies that I'd like to share with you, the word *trust* has come up time and again, along with other vital processes already covered in the recommendations emerging out of the research, notably 'communication'. It is through a variety of systems that schools and parents communicate with each other, and the thoughtful and informed design of these is essential to them being successful I have found, along with a willingness to constantly tweak and adjust those systems when they prove not to be working well with particular parents and to abandon techniques that prove to be unwieldy or widely ineffective.

You will notice that I have also included in the diagram three verbs and a verb phrase, in lower-case text. These are intended to show what it is that schools do to demonstrate to parents, and to encourage them to adopt themselves, the key characteristics that I'm suggesting. For example, accurate *signposting* to other services reveals to the parents the *knowledge* that the school team has acquired by listening carefully to what has been said about their own, or their child's additional needs.

In the rest of this chapter I'm going to take each of the characteristics in turn and explore in a little more detail what they might mean to us in relation to parent partnership in the primary school, and I'll give some hints from my own experience and observations as to what they might consist of practically. I hope that as I do so you will be thinking of your own examples, as well as challenging my personal list of characteristics if you think that any of them should not be included or if you feel that I've omitted other crucial ones. As with the case studies that are to come, these ideas are provisional and intended to provoke and promote further thought on your part as leaders, managers and practitioners.

Respect

I'm starting the unpacking process with *respect* because it strikes me as the attribute that is essential in our first encounter as members of school staff with an individual parent or a group of parents. When, as a headteacher in the middle of a busy term, I showed a prospective parent and their child around the school, they had invariably already been met, and hopefully welcomed, by one of the administrative team, or perhaps a learning mentor, and it was in those first exchanges that the showing of respect would have begun, before my attitude, my body language, my facial expressions and the time and care invested in the task could combine to convey, to a greater or lesser extent, the respect that I was seeking to show in my role as guide. Likewise, the various contributors to a summer term meeting for new reception parents, including myself as headteacher, always took great care to choose a style and approach that we hoped would respect the wide variety of circumstances that the group of parents before us came from. Our choice of inclusive language would have been essential, and again factors like body language, listening ability and overall demeanour must have created a wide variety of initial impressions in our listeners, hopefully engendering a feeling of being respected as they did so.

There are numerous ways in which we can show respect in our dealings with parents, and you could go through every aspect of involvement and engagement that you plan, from the timings of phonics workshops, meetings about internet safety and parents' evening itself, the home learning that you organise and the policies that you write, through to the language that is used on your website or the electronic translation services that you incorporate. How much respect for parental views do you really show as you draft an EHCP for your children with special needs? But perhaps the biggest way in which we can show respect is through our communication with parents, an aspect that I mentioned earlier in this chapter. You will notice that this is not included in my key five characteristics, as I see it as underpinning all of those that I have suggested as vital.

The research makes clear that two-way communication appears to be essential in fostering effective parent partnership, and allowing parents to make the first contribution in a dialogue is important, whether this is about their child alone or a wider issue about policy and practice, such as the ready availability for all pupils of drinking water during the school day. In many schools communication can appear to be flowing out of the school constantly, but how respectful of parents' circumstances and aspirations is it? I found myself that is advisable to allow a couple of representative parents to read, or have read to them, any communications that go out from school on the basis that they would honestly tell me if they thought anything that we had written would be likely to cause offence. I well remember, early in my second headship, meeting a parent at the gate who had got wind of our intention to make a nominal charge towards the cost of producing individual pupil photographs from the Christmas show. 'I can tell you now. There will be trouble if you do that', he informed me with a serious look on his face. We reconsidered the plan and decided to absorb the full cost, and from that moment onwards I felt that particular dad 'had my back' so to speak. His respect for me as a school leader certainly seemed to increase, based on my willingness to listen, and during my four years as his son's headteacher I continued to informally consult him, knowing that he spoke for a group of parents whose lived experiences were vastly different to my own. I didn't always act as he would have wanted, but I like to think that I was always prepared to listen to his point of view.

It seems to me to be sensible for school leaders, and teachers or other staff for that matter, to find parents who will honestly and openly communicate with them so that helpful 'intelligence' can be gathered and acted on, and so that the most favourable strategic decisions can be taken. Now that I am a school governor, I recognise even more clearly the vital role played by well-connected and open parent governors as they network with those they represent, secure in the knowledge that they can share their knowledge about what the parent group as a whole may be thinking on a variety of issues, whilst also encouraging individual parents to bring their concerns or their approval directly to members of staff, including the head, so that the governors don't become the sole conduits of parent voice.

During my time as a headteacher in two contrasting primary schools, my attempts to respect parents ranged from carrying out a BPVS (British Picture Vocabulary Scale) test with a reception pupil whose mum, with a PhD, was as keen to quantify his 'cognitive ability' (in this instance his receptive vocabulary) as I was, to attending a GP clinic with a dad whose seven-year-old son was having trouble with bed-wetting and where I was the only person that they were prepared to have with them on what they saw as a very challenging visit.

I have given some thought as to what might get in the way of building up parental respect, and I suspect that an unwillingness to share power in the professional relationship might be one important factor. During my lifetime I have witnessed the diminution of authority that the medical professions have experienced and probably embraced in the majority of cases. The expansion of the internet in recent years has allowed patients to explore the possible cause of their symptoms before entering the consulting room, embarking on the telephone call or accessing the online meeting space so prevalent during the recent pandemic. I well remember a newly qualified doctor recently asking me what I wanted the outcome to be when I presented with persistent back pain. 'I'd like it to stop hurting please', I ventured, although I recognised and appreciated her willingness for the agenda to be mine as much as hers. I believe that there have been similar changes over the years in the relationship between parents and the teaching profession.

During my first headship, a dad came to me to share the view of his son's optician that he may well have scotopic sensitivity. I was also the interim SENCo at the time, but I hadn't heard of this condition, also called Irlen Syndrome. I could have tried to cover my ignorance, in a vain attempt to maintain my power in the relationship, or I could ask questions about the condition, which is what I chose to do. The dad pointed out some very helpful online references, and within a couple of days I was able to go back to him for a much more informed conversation on my part, and able to signpost him to additional resources, as well as to deploy our external SEN advisor to provide support for his son and to engage our own team appropriately as well.

My experiences of delivering the FAST programme in a number of schools demonstrated the power of a table-based coaching technique. This involves the FAST partners, whether from school or the community, quietly and sensitively making observations and suggestions to parents, during the workshop and family meal activities, when they are having difficulties in managing their children's behaviour. This has the empowering effect of not undermining the parents' place in the family system but instead enabling the parent and child to further develop what might be called a 'tough love' relationship.

Of course, as with the medical profession, there are times when the training and experience of educational professionals are invaluable in the decisions that are made about a child's learning journey and the actions that are taken to ensure the very best possible outcomes for each pupil, and I wouldn't want to suggest that this is not the case. However, a willingness to recognise that 'anyone can have the answer' has stood me in good stead as a school leader and subsequently in my training and consultancy roles, so I would recommend the same for others.

Knowledge

The second vital characteristic that I would like to propose is *knowledge* which I believe is central to building great parent partnership. I remember how easy it was during my own practice as a teacher and school leader to jump to conclusions about families and their situations or circumstances, just as it was all too easy for parents to do the same about school and what went on there. Once again, effective two-way communication underpins knowledge, a time-consuming activity for schools and parents alike, so the better the systems that a school can put in place the more likely that good communication will allow both parties to have as clear a picture as possible of the other. I remember that as positive as our internal annual parent surveys, or our Ofsted online 'Parent View' results, usually were, an area that frequently came up as causing at least some concern was the response to the questions about communication. The Ofsted survey (2019) comments that most relate to communication are currently:

- The school makes me aware of what my child will learn during the year.
- When I have raised concerns with the school they have been dealt with properly.
- The school has high expectations for my child.
- The school lets me know how my child is doing.

Incidentally, I remember that my own annual internal surveys as a headteacher went a good deal further, reflecting a desire on my part, and that of my two staff and governor teams, to include more detail not only on communication systems but also home learning, uptake of ideas generated by parents and so on, as well as an open response on each parent's aspirations for their children in educational and wider terms. In my view the Ofsted survey would benefit from the addition of a specific statement about parent partnership, such as:

- The school encourages me to support my child's learning effectively, or
- The school is committed to developing my effectiveness as a partner in my child's learning.

You can probably come up with something even more succinct and appropriate, and of course, you may well already have done so in your own in-house surveys, as well as adding such statements about particular aspects of parental involvement or engagement as:

- The school communicates effectively with me about day-to-day matters, or
- The school genuinely consults parents before making changes to its systems.

In the last ten years there has been a proliferation of highly efficient online home-school communication systems, some of which we will look at later in the case studies. Had these been available to me during my two headships I'm sure that I would have been looking at a selection of them and potentially implementing one with my staff teams, as long as it could be used to improve communications without putting an undue workload on staff or making unreasonable demands on busy or unconfident parents.

As I mentioned in Chapter 2 a number of management tools are currently available to help with an audit of parental involvement and engagement in your school and I have also added one of my own devising in the appendix, based on a well-tried template for Pupil Premium provision that I've been using with schools for ten years, which incorporates some of the recommendations made by the EEF in their guidance document on the subject (see Chapter 1). It seems to me to be a useful starting point in response to reading this book and could allow you to produce a short but meaningful action plan, aimed at improving your delivery of parent partnership. The knowledge about the current situation in your school should be a powerful precursor to making any improvements necessary, and part of the audit might be an effort to reach as many parents as possible with a specific survey to establish as honestly as possible from parents what they see their needs as in this area, and also what they might have to offer. During my own career in schools I'm pretty sure that I only scratched the surface in finding out what parents had to offer both their own children and perhaps the wider pupil community. Examples that I can remember are parents supporting with educational visits, helping with the school garden, organising and delivering fundraising events and other similarly obvious contributions. I was aware when seeking support for Friday's after-school football club (something I managed to make time for throughout my time as a teacher or school leader) that there were many talented individuals amongst the parent body who could demonstrate and coach skills far better than I could, and I was fortunate to recruit such help, although not always in the numbers that I would have liked. I can only imagine how many talented artists, cooks, writers, musicians, designers, scientists and computer technicians there were out there whom I failed to track down simply because I didn't ask. For this reason, I would now include a survey statement, with a box for the response, along these lines:

- I would be prepared to share with the school my knowledge and skills in the following area(s):

Identifying parents' particular needs in relation to their child's learning has to be approached with great sensitivity and will probably not be achieved easily through questionnaires or surveys. In England, often driven by the need to produce a Pupil Premium Strategy, schools have become familiar with identifying potential 'barriers' to learning, and more recently in the DfE's latest strategy template 'challenges' faced by eligible pupils. These have frequently included examples such as 'lack of reading material at home', 'parents less likely to provide visits to museums' or 'limited access to online resources'. It might be possible to encourage parents to respond openly to statements like the following, again with a box for a response, but possibly in a private and confidential, face-to-face, scribed interview rather than in a widely circulated document:

- The main reasons that I'm not always able to support my child's learning are:
- If I could have more help from school with home learning I would ask for:

Approaching this sort of area with genuine interest strikes me as a further example of respect, and when the results of such conversations are sensitively responded to by the school staff concerned, I foresee that the *trust* between the two participants will naturally increase too. There are a number of excellent examples of this in the case studies that I will share with you in subsequent chapters.

Understanding and empathy

It's one thing to have knowledge about a parent's circumstances but another thing to truly understand and begin to empathise with them. During my person-centred counselling training, undertaken five years ago, and my subsequent practice with clients of all ages, I have become much more aware of the value of empathy in building empowering relationships with other people. It's also crucial that this empathy is communicated clearly to its subject if they are to feel truly understood.

Some time ago I came across an RSA short video clip that I've since used in training events, produced by a cartoonist called Katy Davis, using the spoken words of Brené Brown which attempts (successfully in my view) to explain the difference between empathy and sympathy. You can find it here: www.youtube.com/watch?v=1Evwgu369Jw. In the video Brown says that empathy 'fuels connection' and defines it as 'feeling WITH people'. However, it only has real power to strengthen a relationship when we are able to feedback accurately to others the feelings that we have detected in them, perhaps by paraphrasing at the end of a conversation what we've understood them to have said about themselves and their situation. We often can't do as much to help them as we'd like, but being able to convey that we are in some way aware of what it's like to be in their shoes seems like an important place to start.

During the pandemic many parents came forward with stories about how difficult it was to access online learning with their children, even if they had enough pieces of IT equipment to do so, often because they didn't have the broadband capacity to meet their own needs for work and their children's learning needs. This was incredibly frustrating for those parents, but the schools who were able to listen carefully, appreciate these difficulties and begin to provide vouchers for extra bandwidth, IT equipment from their own resources or government assistance, or paper-based alternatives that were delivered outside of normal hours, proved that they had understood the issues, even if they were often disappointed not to be able to do as much as they would have liked to remedy them.

In my second headship I worked with a mum whose son frequently presented with very challenging, and sometimes violent, behaviour. She had been as pupil in my class during my first year of teaching in Cleethorpes, and we'd established a positive relationship in that time. Now, some 20 years later, she often struggled in multi-agency meetings to control her own emotions about what she was being told by the different agencies, and I could sometimes see her point of view. I remember well, in one such meeting, her frustration at being told that she couldn't be instructed in the safe handling techniques that school staff were able to use if appropriate when her son 'kicked off'. I felt her impotence, given that she believed that such training would help her to keep him safe more effectively than by making it up as she went along, as she was currently doing. I'm not sure how I managed to communicate my empathy with her, but she was adamant during his subsequent time at our local pupil referral unit that she would only attend meetings held at the school where I was headteacher and with me present. If you, too, have had instances where you have managed to make that kind of connection with a parent who has struggled to work with an often-flawed system, or whose circumstances or experiences have become overwhelming, I would suggest that empathy will have been at the heart of the relationship.

In the RSA video referenced above, Brown quotes a nursing scholar, Theresa Wiseman, who looked during the nineteen nineties at a variety of professions in which empathy was relevant, and she came up with the following four qualities of empathy:

1   Perspective taking – the ability to take the perspective of another person (sometimes referred to as 'getting into their frame of reference', or seeing the world as others see it)
2   Staying out of judgement (being non-judgemental, which isn't always easy, as it's a trait that can be very satisfying)
3   Recognising emotion in other people (identifying and understanding their feelings)
4   Communicating that to them (so that they feel less alone and so that their emotions are valued by someone else)

Brown goes on to say that choosing to be empathic might make us vulnerable because we have to get in touch with similar feelings of our own as we try to get alongside the other person. It might be appropriate at this point to disclose personal experiences in a considered way, as this can reinforce the sense of empathy with the listener. However, when an experience that has been shared is especially traumatic, or far beyond our own experience, I particularly like the response suggested by Brown: 'I don't even know what to say right now – I'm just so glad you told me'. I have found in my educational and therapeutic work that taking this approach allows me to recognise, in the words of my counselling trainers, that 'I am enough', even though at that moment there may be nothing I can say or do to help.

Relationship

Over time, if the three preceding principles are in place, a relationship between the school and the parents will develop, consisting of a number of contributing individual relationships that have been forged with particular members of staff, governors, fellow parents and any others who comprise the wider school community. Talking recently to a parent in a Hull primary school, I was intrigued to hear her say that she already had a positive relationship 'with the school' before her daughter started there because she herself had attended it as a child and had thoroughly enjoyed her time there. Of course, if her experience as a parent hadn't matched her recollection of her experience as a pupil then she would have been likely to be disappointed which was not the case from the glowing praise that she felt able to bestow on the current school team, some of whom she'd known as a pupil some 20 years earlier.

A key part of developing a relationship with parents that is likely to encourage them to see themselves as partners in their child's education consists of inviting them to share in the school's decision-making processes. This will range from holding opinion polls on appropriate matters such as vision statements, school uniform, homework, timings of the school day, through to participation in the governance of the school. Informal methods might include coffee mornings, personal invitations to meet with the headteacher or principal to discuss the parent's satisfaction with the school and conversations at the gate involving members of the staff or governor team, as suggested earlier in this chapter.

During my second headship, where I was responsible for overseeing the amalgamation of an 'outstanding' infant school with a 'failing' junior school, I worked with a consultant who suggested that 'you build effective teams by doing good work together'. That notion proved very helpful as I worked to build relationships within the staff teams who were being asked to come together into a single group, and I think it holds true for efforts to welcome parents into the school community. During my time as a deputy headteacher I worked with a small group of parents, one of whom had the necessary construction competences and insurances, to install playground equipment at a much lower cost than had been quoted by the company selling the equipment. I remember the nature of the bonds built that day was deeper than anything I had previously experienced, and during my first headship, I recognised the same quality of relationship forged between staff and parent members of the thriving 'friends' group as I was sweeping the hall floor after the Christmas Fayre.

Parent governors are a key part of the successful development of wider parent partnership, built on their potential to reach out honestly and openly into the school's parent body. I have experienced as a school leader the value of being able to take honest soundings from such networks, and such a web of communication, operating both ways, can foster over a relatively short period of time an almost tangible feeling of relationship between the school leadership and the parents in my experience. I have seen the same effect as chair of governors in a primary school, observing a newly appointed headteacher rapidly building up, for herself and her team, the 'social capital' that I feel is essential to growing a sense of real partnership in children's learning.

I firmly believe that openness and honesty lie at the centre of good relationships, and so transparency in communication is essential as far as I'm concerned, whether through newsletters, texts, tweets, social media posts, meetings or individual conversations. When money has been raised by parents it makes sense to me to ask them first what they would like it to be used for and then to share in reasonable detail how it has been spent. If a parent complains about the behaviour policy in a lengthy email one response might be to share the fact that the policy is constantly under review and to invite them to meet one of the leadership team and a parent governor to discuss possible improvements. During the pandemic, school leaders often found themselves responsible for sharing the current situation with parents in ways that were aimed at building confidence in the COVID precautions in place, whilst maintaining a sense that they were being truthful about the actual risks to health for children attending school.

Trust

Any relationship in life can only be maintained, and perhaps grown, when *trust* is at the heart of it. Once trust is lost relationships can be irrevocably damaged, and this is as much the case in the area of parent partnership as anywhere else in my experience. In the modern school system parents can be seen as customers as in any other business or service users as in any other public sector provision, if you prefer that terminology, and consumer trust is essential whichever perspective you choose to take. Parents have the right to move their child to another school if they are unhappy with its provision, and they will do so as long as there is one within reach. In some instances this is unforeseen and happens without warning. On other occasions parents will voice their concerns or displeasure, possibly going as far as making a complaint, and a period of being 'on notice' follows, during which the school has the chance to prove itself to have listened and reacted positively enough to rebuild the lost trust sufficiently for the child to remain, or not.

You will notice that I have put the word 'trust' in the centre of Figure 3.1 which is intended to indicate that it is created, both ways, by a focus on the other four. We build up trust gradually over time in my experience, but it can be lost in a moment. I well remember the upset caused by copying and pasting errors in school reports, where a child's report included the name of another pupil. When such mistakes had been missed by the teacher, and by me in my proof reading of the reports, parents were understandably concerned that this called into question the accuracy of the whole document, and some even perceived the use of automated or semi-automated systems as evidence that teachers were somehow avoiding their responsibility to report children's progress with sufficient accuracy. I then had to work very hard, not always with success, to persuade dissatisfied parents that the systems in place were designed to make report-writing as manageable as possible, whilst retaining as much rigour as we would want as a school.

Another key area involving a lack of trust is wellbeing, and parents whose child is unhappy through bullying, personality clashes with peers or staff or other significant factors are rightly keen to see that the school has responded. Increased communication at such times, with appropriate sharing of steps taken to resolve issues, can be sufficient to restore parental faith, but there will be occasions when parents feel that a fresh start somewhere else is appropriate.

For some parents their own unfortunate experiences of school make it very hard for them to trust school staff, and this can show, of course, in their approach to school staff. Sensitive and skilful work may alleviate this prejudice enough for an understanding of parent partnership to develop, especially when it takes place initially off-site, or on-site in a room that is easy to reach, and which has been thoughtfully set up with warm decor and simple, encouraging displays that get across an inclusive message. This may also be an opportunity to use a parent buddy whose experience of the school is a positive one and whose lived experience perhaps matches that of the hesitant or reluctant peer. I have seen that approach work powerfully during my time working with the FAST programme, especially during the parent sessions that are a part of it. No school staff are present during this part of the eight evenings that constitute the programme, as the trained community and parent partners facilitate this aspect, over a hot drink. It's in such an environment that I've seen parents begin to open up about their own experiences of school, as well as the challenges they face in their parenting. Such parents can then be encouraged to share their confidential disclosures more widely with appropriate school staff if they wish, such as the parent liaison worker, so that after the programme has finished they can access further support if needed. However, being able to share their feelings in a safe space may be enough to help them begin to move on from the past.

I think parental trust could be seen as the ultimate measure of accountability in a primary school. The Ofsted Parent View survey concludes with this statement:

- I would recommend this school to another parent (yes or no).

Interestingly, this statement is the only one where the response is not graded (between *strongly agree* and *strongly disagree* or *don't know*), possibly reflecting the idea that the parent completing it has to make a judgement about an underlying question which I would state in this way:

- Do you trust this school to take care of your child and enable them (with your support) to become great learners, as well as happy and fulfilled members of society?

It could be argued that the recent pandemic has heightened society's understanding of the responsibility that we undertake in schools to keep pupils healthy, safe and well and to find ways under very challenging circumstances to maintain a high quality of learning for all of them. In that respect I think the world of modern schooling has changed irrevocably, although hopefully with some positive tools to take forward in deepening the trust that parents and schools have in each other.

Supporting activities

You will remember that I am suggesting four supporting activities, the verbs and verb phrase in Figure 3.1, and I'd like to define them briefly in this section. They will be elaborated on more fully in the case studies that follow.

- **Being transparent** – wherever possible schools should be *open* and *honest* with parents, in line with the Nolan Principles, advocated by the United Kingdom government.
- **Signposting** – schools have a duty to inform parents about well-researched additional services, whether statutory or voluntary, that can support them with their own needs and those of their children.
- **Listening** – this strand of a school's approach with parents has been woven through the fabric of this chapter and is essential to encouraging parental involvement and engagement.
- **Delivering** – nothing undermines parental trust as quickly as a perception that promises have not been kept, so carrying out agreed actions, and following up on them if appropriate, are essential if trust is to be built and relationships developed.

Key ideas in this chapter

- A whole-school, principled approach to parental involvement and engagement is required if parent partnership is to be promoted effectively.

Principles for practice in parental involvement and engagement 47

- A 'default setting' of respect for parents, and the contributions they can make to support their children's learning, should lead to them feeling included in the education process.
- When a school has good knowledge of its current performance in this area, combined with awareness of the nature of individual parents' needs and resources, it is able to take the steps necessary for continuous improvement.
- Staff empathy and understanding are very likely to enable supportive and empowering relationships to develop with parents so that opportunities for partnership around children's learning are taken up when offered.
- Where these principles or characteristics are embedded in the school's approach mutual trust should grow and be sustained.
- Strategic planning by the school will ensure that key actions such as being transparent, signposting, listening and delivering are in place.

This is not intended to be a complete list, so you might like to add your own key ideas here from your reading in this chapter and any further thoughts about earlier material.

Conversation starters

Here are some follow-up questions to help you develop your own thinking about the ideas that I've proposed and any others that have been important to you in relation to securing effective parent partnership as widely as possible.

- What evidence can we find in our school for the principles and characteristics described?
- How seriously do we take the notion of parent voice?
- How well do we know our customers (service users), and how much thought have we given to responding to their ideas about their children's schooling, education and wider learning?
- What steps could we take in the next year, and the following two years, to strengthen our commitment to the principles, characteristics and behaviours that we believe are required to foster parent partnership at our school?
- To what extent are these intentions included in our School Improvement (or Development) Plan?

Chapter 3 reference list

Ofsted. Available at: www.gov.uk/guidance/ofsted-parent-view-toolkit-for-schools#ofsted-parent-view-questions (Accessed 20.6.22)

4 Case studies

The methodology for selecting the schools, collecting evidence about their parent partnership practice and presenting it in an organised form

After nearly ten years working as an educational consultant all over England, visiting over two hundred schools and working in training events with many times that number I have seen, or heard about, parent partnership in action in a large number of schools, often in relation to the use of Pupil Premium funding, which has been my main area of interest in that time. When I decided to write this book I envisaged fleshing it out with case studies from a few of those schools, not to set them up as paragons, representing perfection, but as exemplars, or typical examples that have elements worthy of imitation in my opinion. When I approached each headteacher or principal I explained that I was hoping to present material that would get my readers thinking and that might therefore stimulate improvements in the parental involvement and engagement processes of other schools, with the accompanying benefits to pupils' learning.

It is in that spirit that I have written Chapters 5 to 9 which I have structured so that you can track each school's ethos and methods across the five key characteristics or principles described in Chapter 3. You might decide to follow one school at a time, by reading about them in each chapter in turn, or you may prefer just to read the chapters in sequence, getting a wider sense of each of my suggested principles as you proceed.

I have worked with some of the schools for over five years, and others I have become involved with only during the last year. I have chosen six schools in very different contexts and from a range of places in their Ofsted inspection journeys. Their catchments are varied in terms of ethnicity and levels of disadvantage, and the group includes one infant school and one special school.

Once the schools were selected I arranged to either visit them, where geography allowed, or conduct a virtual meeting, on one or more occasions, so that I could have conversations with school leaders, teachers, other practitioners and parents. Figure 4.1 provides a thumbnail description of each of the schools, along with a list of the staff members, first names only, who kindly gave up their time to share their understanding of what works in their schools, the challenges that they have overcome and to some extent the ways in which they feel they could further improve or widen parent partnership. According to my colleagues this last feature of the way that I worked with them has invariably given them real food for thought about how they can press on to develop their practice, even if the resulting plans and ideas haven't made it onto the pages that follow.

Case studies 49

Identifier	Rathfern	Chiltern	Brunel	Carrington	Littlecoates	Beaumont Hill
Full name and Local Authority	Rathfern Primary School, Lewisham, London	Chiltern Primary School, Kingston upon Hull	Brunel Primary and Nursery and Academy, Plymouth	Carrington Infant School, Buckinghamshire	Littlecoates Primary Academy, North East Lincolnshire	Beaumont Hill Academy, Darlington
Academy Trust	Community school	Thrive Co-operative Learning Trust	Bridge Multi-Academy trust	Community school	Wellspring Academy Trust	The Education Village Academy Trust
Contributing staff	Naheeda (Headteacher) Daniela (Inclusion Manager and DSL), Linda (Lead TA), Chantelle (AHT, EYFS Lead, Nursery teacher), Rose (Lead TA)	Kath (Executive Headteacher), Jacqui (Head of School), Claire (Assistant Head), Lisa (Pastoral Support Worker and Deputy DSL)	Suzanne (Headteacher), Paul (Assistant Head)	Kate (Headteacher) Rachael (Deputy Head) Anna (EYFS Lead)	Neville (Principal) Emma (Vice Principal) Kate (SENDCo) Dawn (Office manager)	Caroline (Executive Principal) Helen (Assistant Head) Kirsty (Assistant Head, EYFS and Primary lead, Quality of education)
Number and age of pupils	498 (3 to 11)	465 (3 to 11)	298 (2 to 11)	166 (5 to 7)	188 (2 to 11)	268 (2 to 19)
Proportion eligible for FSM (Free School Meals)	24 percent	43 percent	23 percent	27 percent	47 percent	51 percent
Meeting method used	Virtual	Face-to-face	Virtual	Virtual	Face-to-face	Virtual

For more information about the schools please visit: www.get-information-schools.service.gov.uk/

Figure 4.1 Schools chosen as case studies

The individual or group interviews were initially based on a question template which I devised with reference to the EEF guidance document described in Chapter 1. Each of the schools was provided with a prompt document (see Figure 4.2) which you might like to apply to your own school as a strategic tool, and the discussions were all recorded digitally so that I would have additional material to add to the notes that I made as each conversation proceeded. The task that I then set myself was to take the evidence collected and organise it according to the five key principles from Chapter 3 into the chapters that follow. This is not intended to be a scientific or statistically robust methodology but simply a way to present what I found in a way that is accessible and informative to you the reader. In doing so, I invite you also to keep in mind any insights gained from the literature review in Chapter 1, the model proposed in Chapter 2 and any ideas of your own that you have come up with as you've read the book so far. I hope that through reading the next five chapters of the book you are able to come up with helpful suggestions or questions to bring to bear on the ways in which you and your parents interact so that your strategic thinking is stimulated and informed by the process. You will find that I have attempted something similar myself in each of the five 'key-ideas-in-this-chapter' sections, but your own learning 'take-aways' will be just as valid no doubt, given your knowledge of your own school context.

You may feel that I have been rather arbitrary in my allocation of different aspects of each school's parent partnership efforts to one chapter or another, and it's possible that I could have been more systematic. However, in summing up the key points at the end of each chapter I will hopefully explain my thinking in including the various accounts where I have, and in the final analysis you are welcome to draw your own conclusions as to which of my proposed principles is being exemplified, or even to decide that a characteristic of your own devising is at play. If I have made you think more deeply about your own situation in school in relation to parent partnership, and provided you with some relevant vignettes to inform your school's improvement planning, then these chapters will have served their purpose.

Parent Partnership prompt questions based on the EEF guidance

1) What steps have you taken in the last few years to critically review (and improve) how you work with parents, not just how you involve them in the life and work of your school but also how you encourage them to be engaged in the learning of pupils in school and, especially, at home?
2) What practical strategies are you able to provide to support learning at home, how widely have they been taken up and how well are they working do you think?
3) How do you tailor your two-way communications with parents, in ways that encourage positive dialogue between them and their children about learning, and lead to positive home-school conversations too?
4) Are there ways in which you sensitively and inclusively (perhaps through a universal approach) offer more sustained and intensive support for parental involvement and engagement where you or the parents feel it's needed?

Figure 4.2 Parent Partnership prompt questions based on the EEF guidance

Of course, much of this book was written during the COVID-19 pandemic, or in its aftermath, and school practices around parental involvement and engagement have been massively affected by the experiences of parents and school staff during that difficult period. You will see in the following accounts very practical ways in which both groups of people worked tirelessly, and often ingeniously, to overcome the barriers to learning that were created, as well as to learn from the often unforeseen 'silver-lining' opportunities that presented themselves.

I found, unsurprisingly I suppose, that learnt a lot from carrying out the research interviews and visits, refining my methodology to some extent as I went along. One of the advantages of virtual meetings was the relative ease with which we were able to get a number of people together, and it was possible to revisit schools efficiently if I felt that more information might be beneficial. The basic process, whether carried out virtually or in person, was roughly the same for each of the schools, and I have indicated in Figure 4.1 how my interactions were conducted. It consisted of:

- Meet school leaders for a voice-recorded interview of about one hour to have a conversation about parent partnership, based on four prompts that were sent to the school beforehand (approximately one hour).
- Meet a group of parents to ask them individually or in small groups what they thought their school was doing well to promote their involvement or engagement, and make notes to include direct quotes where possible (one hour).
- Listen to the recordings of the discussions with staff and make notes, under the headings of each of the chapters, to allocate (in as balanced a way as possible) each piece of information to the prime characteristic or principle that I felt was being exhibited, often by both school staff and parents (three hours).
- Write up in full the notes for each school, including the parent voice that I had captured, under each chapter heading and then send them to the head or principal of each one to ask for any changes that they would like to see before publication (there were very few, all of which I was happy to make) (five hours).
- Reassemble all of the 30 sections into the next five chapters.

I have included the timings for the different parts of the process to give you some idea of the total commitment that you would probably need from an independent colleague of your own choice (ten hours or so), should you be in a school leadership position yourself, and if you think you might learn something from the experience of being on the receiving end (or perhaps the delivery side) of such a study. I will say a bit more about this in Chapter 10, by which time you will hopefully have read a lot more of the material that I was able to generate with the contributing schools.

Key ideas in this chapter

- How I chose the schools to work with for the case study.
- What my methodology was, and how I have structured the next five chapters.
- How you might like to use part are all of this methodology to evaluate your own practice or that of your whole school.

Case studies

This is not intended to be a complete list, so you might like to add your own key ideas here from your reading in this chapter and any further thoughts about earlier material:

Conversation starters

Here are some follow-up questions to help you develop your own thinking about the ideas that I've proposed and any others that have been important to you in relation to securing effective parent partnership as widely as possible.

- What might be the better way to read the next five chapters – a school at a time or a principle or characteristic at a time (i.e. reading the chapters in order)?
- How will I record my thoughts as I read the case studies? Am I going to squiggle in pencil (or even pen!) under the interesting bits, or will I make separate notes so that I can pass the book on to someone else when I've read it?
- Would it be helpful to undertake something similar to this 'review' in my school, either for my own professional benefit in the role that I have or for the organisation as a whole?
- If so, who might I ask to conduct it, and could I keep the cost down by offering to conduct a reciprocal visit or virtual meeting?

5 Respect

Ways in which schools seek to show respect to parents, and encourage respect in return

Rathfern

Since coming to the school 14 years ago the headteacher Naheeda has worked tirelessly to encourage all members of the school's staff team, and governing body, to challenge what she calls a 'deficit view on race and class'. This has required patient coaching during that time so that staff members are able to model to children and their parents a view that sees potential rather than problems and looks to change the system rather than look for blame in individual learners when success doesn't come readily.

The underlying message in staff-parent interactions at Rathfern is intended to be, for each and every person, 'You matter to me and your child matters to me'. Naheeda firmly believes that this moral purpose is essential to creating successful partnerships with parents around their child's learning. Reflecting on one relationship with a particularly challenging father she remembers heated exchanges at first, leading by the end of that child's journey through the school with her taking part in the Year 6 leaving performance, and the dad's open appreciation of all that the school had done for her. It seems to me that the persistent and unflinching commitment that Naheeda showed to including that parent paid off through the clarity of her ambition for his child's learning outcomes and sense of belonging.

Staff at Rathfern see supporting families with the lower tiers of Maslow's hierarchy of needs – physiological needs such as food, water, warmth, rest, security and safety, as well as psychological needs such as self-esteem – as fundamental to respecting them as subsequent supporters of their children's learning, so they work hard to provide for these needs in any ways that they can within the school and its resources, or signpost parents to those organisations that can help them.

Another way in which respect is shown is through initiatives like 'language of the month' to reflect the hugely diverse backgrounds and cultures of the families served by the school. Parents are encouraged to volunteer to help with learning in the school in wide range of areas, from demonstrating needlework to bringing a baby into the class to support learning in science. Other parents are invited to come into school to share information about the paid and unpaid jobs that they do in the local community, and the qualifications, skills and aptitudes needed to carry them out. All of these ways of involving parents serve to build up their feelings of self-worth and belonging, as well as showing the respect that teachers and others staff have for their lived experiences. It doesn't seem a huge leap to me for a parent to move

DOI: 10.4324/9781003232070-5

from this sense of acceptance to wanting to engage more deeply in developing those conversations at home that will support and encourage their child's learning. In addition, being involved in even the slightest way in delivering education could be instrumental in developing a greater respect for the school's work and those professionals who deliver it.

During the pandemic many key staff, such as the inclusion manager, found that offering virtual meetings increased the uptake by parents as it was easier for many of them to participate than coming into school, given that they often had younger children at home. The efficiency of her work in reviewing the progress of SEN children was much greater, as was her ability to meet with professionals from other services, such as social workers. The school's leadership team is hoping to keep up this virtual offer where appropriate, whilst retaining the face-to-face meetings that continued to a limited extent throughout the lockdowns, with suitable precautions in place.

When Naheeda and her team started trying to engage parents more they discovered that when food was offered as part of a group meeting, activity or workshop the attendance was higher and the outcomes better. As one of them put it, especially given the school community's multi-ethnic mix, 'food is the universal language'. They have also found that offering parents opportunities to share food from their own cultural repertoire has often led to them feeling respected by school staff and their parental peers, with corresponding improvements in self-confidence and deeper feelings of belonging.

To summarise the Rathfern ethos in terms of parent partnership the collective staff view appears to be 'We meet parents where they're at', not judging them if at all possible and avoiding phrases to describe them such as 'hard to reach'. This approach has clearly paid dividends over the years that it has been in place.

Figure 5.1 A pop-up street café at Rathfern

Chiltern

When Chiltern became part of the Thrive Co-operative Learning Trust four years ago there was a restructure of the school's leadership team, with Kath coming in as executive headteacher and Jacqui stepping up into the role of head of school. It quickly became apparent that the previous leadership team's approach had been rather *ad hoc*, so the newly-formed team was keen to put something more coherent in place. Respect for the parents was paramount, based largely on the realisation that the widespread deprivation affecting the catchment area had led to parents needing the kind of support that the school was well-placed to offer. Trying to make a difference to the levels of disadvantage experienced by many families had to be done with respect but with a clear commitment to the central notion that 'if the parents are okay then the children will be too', as one of the current team so succinctly puts it.

A drop-in food bank with the alliteratively engaging title 'Chat and Choose', centred on tea or coffee and a biscuit, was quickly put in place in a newly created community hub, with the choice of title deliberately intended to respect the need for parents to feel good about accessing the food on offer. In exchange for a pound the refreshments and a listening staff ear were provided, as well as the chance to meet and converse with other parents. While parents were in the room they were invited to look in the 'Chiltern's Pantry', as it's called, to see if anything to support their child's nutrition caught their eye. Parents readily took to the offer, and over subsequent years a wide range of activities have been offered, including visits from local PCSOs (Police Community Support Officers), a breast cancer awareness charity, outreach events from adult education providers and a cartoon drawing workshop.

Today, the hub is full every single Thursday, and staff are convinced that if 20 parents attend at least 20 others who are friends and acquaintances will have cascaded to them by word of mouth any information or ideas that have been given. In addition, 75 food parcels are collected each week by parents, 'come rain or shine' as Kath puts it. The school featured in a local news bulletin in May 2022, with parents accessing the Chiltern's Pantry speaking with real gratitude about what the school is doing to support them through what was being called at the time a 'cost of living crisis'. As the presenter states at the end of the piece 'places like this will be there to soften the blow' to families of struggling to feed themselves adequately. The school's organisational effort on parents' behalf builds up goodwill with parents, with positive attitudes to schooling and education also being strengthened in the process the school hopes.

One area of very practical support for parents and their children, respectfully offered to all, is the opportunity for parents to hire a bike and a helmet for a year so that their child can learn to ride. It is this sort of approach that has led to some very pleasing parent survey responses, including in the academic year 2018-19 an Ofsted Parent View set of 174 completed surveys (from a roll of 465 children). The school gathered this huge quantity of data by making IT equipment and support available to parents during parents' evenings, and other key times of day, in a concerted effort to collect as much parent voice as possible. Post-COVID, staff intend to repeat the activity, hopefully at similar scale. At about the same time, Ofsted stated in a report: 'The school's ethos of being "a caring, cooperative community with high aspirations" is woven through the fabric of the school'.

Another respectful approach is the Uniform Swap Shop which allows parents to engage in the mutually helpful opportunity to bring in items if uniform of one size and swap them for something bigger, another way in which the school seeks to avoid parents feeling stigmatised by taking up money-saving schemes. The school has seen attendance rise to close to national figures, although this was affected as in many schools by the pandemic, and one way of recognising great attendance from individual pupils has been the ice-rink reward visits which parents enrol their children on, in recognition of the contribution they have made to them being in school consistently. Chat and Choose has also been a forum at which parents have sometimes felt confident enough to share ways in which they can offer knowledge, talents and skills to the school for the benefit of other children and the wider community.

Brunel

Having it had a turbulent few years Ofsted graded the school as inadequate so, in addition to responding to the COVID-19 pandemic, staff and governors have also had to focus on rapid school improvement. Brunel is now well and truly on the road to a judgement of 'good' at its next full inspection, according to the most recent monitoring visit report from the inspectorate. High-quality support from the Bridge Schools multi-academy trust has been a contributory factor, as has the hard work and dedication of the staff, governors and, of course, the pupils. Throughout this journey Suzanne, the school's headteacher, is grateful to the parents for what she has described in the local press as their 'ongoing support'. This support has only been sustained and developed through the respect shown by members of the school community to all of its parents, as valued users of the school's educational and wider services, and consequently parents' respect for what the school has spent the last four years striving to achieve appears to be growing in return.

Assistant head, Paul, who has responsibility for Pupil Premium expenditure in the school, and more broadly in the Trust, suggests that when you are considering parental engagement and involvement it's a matter of identifying as carefully as possible what individual parents aren't able to offer in support of their children's learning and then 'plugging the gaps' as he puts it. In order to discover what role the school can play in partnership with its parents Paul explains that 'getting out there' is what key staff at Brunel do, with what he calls the 'school gate smile'. The school campus is a large and complex one, with three separate entrances, each of which is overseen by a member of the senior leadership team at the beginning and end of the school day. Each member of the team has a regular spot so that they get to know the families who use their gate, but in future they will be rotating periodically so that Suzanne especially is able to interact with everyone over the year.

Currently, Paul has responsibility for the entrance near the local library and its car park, which he performs a circuit of each time the initial rush has died down so that he can pick up any slightly late arrivals or departures and respectfully enquire as to why this might be the case. As he puts it, 'I like to have a chat with the parents', and his ready smile and engaging manner serve him well in initiating short but meaningful conversations. Paul returned quite recently to the school as an assistant head, after a period of some years working in another trust school, and he picked up some hesitancy in the staff to go outside and meet parents, given the bumpy road that the school had experienced lately. He understands the value of being proactive, of starting discussions with parents, on the basis that he can only help with issues or receive praise on behalf of the school if he knows what has happened and what they are thinking about it. For those situations where an incident in school has upset a parent, Paul sees his intervention as potentially 'nipping it in the bud' and allowing him to begin the processes of reconciliation and collaboration as quickly as possible.

On reaching the gate Paul's technique is to 'make a beeline for someone who looks receptive, and get talking'. From this opening he is then able to branch out into conversation with other parents or be available for interruptions from those who want to initiate a chat for whatever reason. He's aware of a small number of such 'friendly faces' in his particular group of parents but tries hard not to allow this familiarity to become too consuming of his time when others feel the need to talk. Paul recognises that not everyone has his natural aptitude for engaging with people they don't know well but believes that the vast majority of parents appreciate his availability at the gate, and that of his two colleagues, and he feels that anyone who would like to try adopting what many school leadership teams see as good practice will generally be met with a positive response, as long as it's done respectfully.

Such brief encounters have frequently led to a deepening of a parent's involvement in the school, such as one recent conversation with a mum who Paul didn't realise was a baker. She offered to make some red, white and blue cakes for the children in his class, in celebration of The Queen's platinum jubilee, an offer which he was delighted to accept. Importantly, since this contribution to school life, Paul has gone on to have further conversations with her

Figure 5.2 Brunel's assistant headteacher with a parent

about learning-related matters, and their mutual respect for each other has inevitably grown out of his valuing of her skill. As Paul succinctly puts it, 'I didn't know she could do that until we got talking', which could perhaps be true of the vast majority of the parents any of us has ever worked with.

Other evidence of the respect shown to parents at Brunel includes the lengths that the SENDCo goes to in order to share fully and openly the 'assess-plan-do-review' processes that are at the heart of the school's work with the parents of children with special educational needs and disabilities. One example of the many outcomes of this collaboration is the use of 'Theraplay', where the visiting practitioner works not only with the child but also the parents so that they are appropriately involved in the programme.

Carrington

When Kate joined Carrington as headteacher she did so just six months after the beginning of a pandemic, so at the time of writing she is only just beginning to see the school under something like normal conditions, now that the lockdowns and unusually high staff and pupil absences are a thing of the past. This inevitably made it difficult to communicate readily with parents and to show respect for them in what might be considered the traditional ways. It was also very difficult for her to discover how the staff had traditionally done this themselves so that she could begin to bring her own influence to play on how parental involvement and engagement were to be approached.

Anecdotal evidence from members of the school community about the quality of the educational offer during the first lockdown wasn't as good Kate would have hoped. 'I wanted Carrington to be the best', as she puts it, and so it was improved in the second major lockdown, with all those children who couldn't be in school being offered online learning, as well as live online teaching sessions, something that parents are apparently still talking about a year later. This wasn't necessarily the case in other schools, especially in Key Stage One, and those parents who were still able to bring their children into school were also hugely appreciative of the contribution this made to them being able to carry on as working families. Since the pandemic eased the school hasn't attempted to maintain a blended approach to schooling, largely because it isn't thought to be helpful to provide self-isolating pupils with an online link to real-life lessons, in the way that it might be for older children.

Staff at Carrington have constantly provided support to many parents with what's happening in their child's life, through informal conversations, emails, telephone calls and so on, but the deputy head, Rachael, also works with specific families in a bespoke way, for example by modelling play, and the language around it, to one mum during weekly sessions. There is a limited capacity for this kind of work, but where the need is particularly high the sensitive welcome extended by the school, and the determination to provide what parents require, speaks volumes about the respect that Rachael and other staff routinely have for the families they seek to serve.

In her previous school leadership role in Qatar Kate had experienced considerable success with a parent group that met with her on the site during the school day, but this clearly wasn't possible when she first arrived in High Wycombe. Subsequently, as restrictions eased, she implemented a similar idea, but wasn't happy that it was including as many different individual parents as she had hoped. Consequently, the half-termly 'Class Parents' group has moved online, with a virtual meeting being advertised well in advance in a variety of school communications, stating when Kate will be available and for how long, if anyone would like to join her. The meeting is billed as an opportunity for parents to discuss with her any positives about their experiences of the school, as well as their ideas for any aspects of school life that might be developed. As she puts it when talking to parents, 'Your eyes are looking at things differently to mine'. Examples of topics that have come up recently have included uniform, meals and traffic around the school. The group has had up to 25 parents in attendance and has so far had the positive and informal feel that Kate was hoping for. Their conversations are reported in the subsequent school newsletter so that the whole parent community has access to what has been discussed and potentially proposed. Although Kate sees this as 'keeping the wheels oiled' in the school-parent interface it seems clear that her attempt to garner parent opinion and ideas in this way is a respectful mechanism, characteristic of the wider Carrington approach to parent partnership.

Littlecoates

Neville became principal of the school a little under a year before an Ofsted inspector wrote the following during a short inspection:

> Since you became Principal in September 2018, you have quickly gained the trust and respect of parents, staff and pupils.

When talking to Neville and members of the staff team it quickly becomes clear that, far from sitting back on this affirmation, he has shown a relentless commitment to build on the parental trust and respect secured, in ways that seek to constantly improve partnership throughout the parent community. In a short briefing document prepared for my research visit to Littlecoates he states, 'We believe that for our children to thrive, their parents need to thrive'. He goes on to suggest, with characteristic sensitivity, that many of the school's parents are 'not in the best position to support home learning'. He describes the school's main priority in improving how it works with parents as putting 'a lot of energy into helping them to overcome the barriers that are impeding their capacity to support their children's learning'.

As with so many schools in the current economic climate, a food bank has been established to support its most needy families, with the alliterative and respectful title Littlecoates Larder, which two parents have gradually become more involved in organising and supervising. School staff and the local area's funded NSPCC link workers attend regularly because it provides a great opportunity for them to chat with the parents visiting the larder and to break down any barriers to perceived authority figures that might exist. The school's vision for the future is to expand the facility into a full-blown community hub, the Littlecoates Lounge (more alluring alliteration), where parents will be able to come and do their washing as well, perhaps enjoying a conversation with others while waiting for the cycle to finish. Coffee mornings are also held there, as is the school's breakfast club, sponsored by Greggs.

Another resource provided in the sizeable school grounds is a rapidly growing nature reserve, developed by a 'green-influencers' group of pupils, recognising the fact that many of the children have limited garden space at home and that their parents don't always have the resources to make trips into the local countryside. A parent of one of the school's Year 4 pupils has designed, created and now maintains a number of gardens around the site. She offered her services one evening when she picked her child up from a club, and the school was happy to accept her generous proposal. Her gardening knowledge and expertise have been what Vice Principal Emma describes as a 'godsend', with each class having a space to grow plants in and staff now having someone who can answer the question 'What would you plant here?' Whilst the school has no formal method for auditing parents' ability to support its educational efforts, Emma believes that this willingness to accept safeguarded contributions reflects Littlecoates's openness to parent partnership offers.

In the main entrance is a well-run and eye-catching 'pocket money bookshop', replete with a pre-owned selection of children's books for swapping, a range of new books priced at one pound and a collection of adult books that can just be taken by any parents who would like some reading material themselves. In having the resource in such an accessible location the school recognises that parents might want their child to read at home but might not have the money to buy books.

Neville is passionate about constantly developing further community links, and he has spent a number of evenings attending strategy meetings at the West Marsh community centre, serving as it does the area of Grimsby in which Littlecoates is situated. This visibility on the local 'patch' is a hallmark of his leadership and perhaps another way in which he shows his respect for the families he serves, as well as his willingness to engage in dialogue with them, and with those who might be able to improve their children's life chances.

One result of the lockdown is that all the children now have their own Chromebook, with QR codes to make access as easy as possible, combined with almost universal use of Google Classroom and Google Docs so that everyone can attempt any homework that has been set.

Parent voice is taken very seriously, with annual surveys completed, and the results widely publicised in the school foyer, in one of the weekly newsletters, as well as on the school website. If any follow-up actions are needed then the school's parent governors are responsible for taking a lead. As with everything else under this heading there can be little doubt that under Neville's inspirational leadership the whole staff team at Littlecoates are well-versed in demonstrating their respect for parents as partners in their children's wellbeing and learning.

Beaumont Hill

This special school is part of a large campus called The Education Village in Darlington, and although it educates children with a wide range of special educational needs and disabilities from the age of two to 19 years it has a discrete early years and primary phase with which I have worked to give some thought to the particular aspects of primary-age parental involvement and engagement that are a consideration for the special school sector.

During a virtual interview with Helen, the assistant principal who has recently returned to the school from a secondment to a local partner special school, and Kirsty, assistant principal with responsibility for early years and the primary phase, I explore with them how they have addressed what they both recognise as a key part of the educational provision at Beaumont Hill. Helen is passionate about parent partnership, applying for the precise assistant principal role that offered an opportunity to take responsibility developing it further. Kirsty had previously led on this area of school life, so they are ideally placed between them to inform me about recent developments and current practice.

Both recognise the need to show respect to their parents, especially in the early stages of building up a working relationship. They suggest that communication channels in special schools tend to be more individually bespoke, given the particular needs of the children concerned and the relatively high ratios of staff to pupils and, therefore, to parents too. An example of this has been the willingness that staff have shown to keeping remote meetings as an option now that face-to-face parents' evenings are back after the COVID-19 pandemic. They recognise that childcare is a problem for many, so offering this facility is very helpful to those who wish to choose it, and shows them how much the school values the partnership interactions that they afford to both parties. The school's own evidence suggests that historically less-engaged parents are more likely to attend virtual meetings, including EHCP (education, health and care plan) conferences and annual reviews, so these may become the default for some families, and face-to-face meetings will become an alternative where suitable.

Kirsty explains that the school launched its parents' Facebook page just before COVID struck, and staff immediately noticed that parents that they wouldn't normally see face-to-face quickly began to use it. This in-house platform has since been an excellent mechanism for sharing social stories that parents can use to reduce the stress levels of those children who need them, on subjects that have included the pandemic itself and, more recently, events in Ukraine. During the pandemic parents picked up a lot of strategies from watching teachers working directly online with their children, on activities like social stories, and a number of these are now available on the in-house platform.

Staff show considerable respect for their parents by producing videos to support home learning, such as reading stories or delivering phonics inputs, and these are also readily available in the virtual learning environment. It's a strategy that began during the lockdowns but which will definitely be retained, as it enables those parents who don't have the understanding or who can't read, or in other ways aren't equipped themselves to deal with the academic challenge of the work, to support their children by sitting with them to watch the videos. According to Helen and Kirsty this reduces the pressure on such parents, who then feel that 'it's not down to them to deliver'. This approach has not only impacted on parent engagement in support for home learning but also on the pupils' academic progress.

The school is also steering parents towards taking accredited online course from a local college. As Helen puts it, many of the parents don't just want to be known as 'Mam'. Many of them, especially the mums it seems, have given up their own careers to become carers, and she feels that a lot of them would make great teaching assistants, chiefly because of the skills they've acquired from this caring, supporting parental role. School staff are looking into helping more parents to attend maths and English courses so that they can support their own child, as well as to potentially open future training and employment doors for themselves. Helen can imagine that allowing the Beaumont Hill English and maths leads to support these parents with coursework for that training would be desirable, but she's far from sure that the capacity would be there to do so, even if it would benefit the children, too, in the longer run. As respectful as this would be in relation to the parents' learning needs, in the real world it is arguably not the school's responsibility to provide what reduced adult-learning services no longer offer on-site, as has been the case in the past.

Key ideas in this chapter

When reflecting on the six accounts above, I have tried to pick out some of the actions and approaches that appear to have fostered mutual respect in the parent-school interface most effectively. Some of them have been put forward by more than one of the schools chosen. As with other chapters, there is space at the bottom of the list for you to add your own observations. You may also like to look back at the suggested model in Chapter 2 to see if any of them can be mapped onto the diagram that I have shared.

- Communicate to parents that they and their children matter.
- Be clear about the school's moral purpose through adopting a clear and tangible ethos statement.
- Support families with all their needs, recognising that if parents thrive, so will their children.
- Recognise and value all backgrounds and cultures.
- Retain or adapt effective engagement and involvement systems developed during the COVID pandemic.
- Where possible meet parents 'where they are at' without judging them.
- Use parents who attend events to cascade information to their peers and build up broader goodwill.
- Gather parent voice and respond to it, recognising the value of their unique perspective and sharing the outcomes widely.
- Celebrate and reward parent and pupil successes.
- Ensure that key staff, including leaders and managers, are readily available to parents.
- Value parents' knowledge and skills by using them to support educational and extra-curricular activities (with safeguarding).
- Work transparently with parents in relation to their children's learning, especially for those with SEND.
- Enable parents to understand and overcome the barriers that impede their capacity to support their children's learning.
- Be prepared to design bespoke communication systems that work for individual parents where needed.
- Share learning resources openly with parents, including through virtual learning environments.
- Signpost parents to training courses and other personal development opportunities.

You might like to add your own key ideas here from your reading in this chapter and any further thoughts about earlier material:

Conversation starters

Here are some follow-up questions to help you develop your own thinking about the ideas that I've proposed and any others that have been important to you in relation to securing effective parent partnership as widely as possible.

- In what ways do I as a practitioner, and we as a school, show our parents that we respect them and their children?
- How do we encourage parents to respect the school's staff, systems and processes in return?
- How might we improve these, based on the ideas and examples shared in this chapter and a wider reading of this book and other sources?

6 Knowledge

The extent to which the school knows the nature and quality of its parent partnership work, the needs of its parents, and the steps it takes to encourage parents to know what the school offers and how they can access and contribute to it

Rathfern

When talking to Naheeda and key staff about the area of parental involvement and engagement it is apparent that they share a lifelong commitment to working with the 'community', a word that comes up a lot. Those staff who have worked in the school for many years have built up an intimate knowledge of the local community, but when Naheeda became headteacher staff collaborated to come up with five core values which are clearly articulated on the school website, not just as a collection of unrelated aspirations but linked to a coherent process by which a 'sustainable and equitable future for all' is to be built. These core values are:

- Respect each other.
- Always question your best.
- Take responsibility.
- Help and care about each other.
- Everyone matters.

The School Improvement Plan is built around the 'Three Ms' as Naheeda, and the rest of her team, are proud to explain when we talk about the school's strategic thinking. Moral purpose, metacognition and malleable intelligence are the ideas that provide a framework for the school's intentions and are shared rigorously with parents through workshops, newsletters and other means. Having determined what the three underlying ideas mean to them, school staff encourage parents to apply them in the discussions they have with their children about learning and in the support and encouragement they offer them. Workshops are provided, in which they are explained in more detail, especially metacognition, and the incremental (rather than fixed) nature of intelligence.

As the school was rolling out its parental involvement and engagement systems it became increasingly apparent that initial teacher training, and learning support, courses had very little content on parent partnership, so Naheeda approached her local authority to offer to fill this gap with some training aimed at newly qualified teachers (NQTs), and she is building up a set of resources that have been used widely already in Lewisham it seems.

DOI: 10.4324/9781003232070-6

In order to determine as thoroughly as possible what the parents' own needs are the school operates an open-door policy, aiming to be both proactive in seeking out the information they need, as well as reactive to what they discover when they've done so. One of the current Lead TAs was involved in the selection process that brought Naheeda to Rathfern and remembers being struck then by her commitment to parent engagement. In the early days school staff met some parents off-site in a local café to remove barriers to communication. Over a relatively short period of time the school put in place termly family-learning workshops and home-learning clubs, with participation in these events gradually growing over that period, until these approaches were embedded. Regular changes to what is offered are now built in so that the offer doesn't become stale or too repetitive. The school prides itself in making every effort to provide evidence-informed learning and to encourage it at home, with the latest thinking on emotional regulation and executive function being carefully researched and enthusiastically shared with parents in as many different ways as possible.

Another highly-rated aspect of Naheeda's headship from the outset was, by all accounts, an observation by a great many parents, shared in conversations with existing staff, that 'The headteacher knows my child's name'. This knowledge of children as individuals, demonstrated at the school gate, of course, as well as in other ways, was a massive indicator that the developing ethos of the school had individuality at its core and went a long way to proving to parents that their child and its needs really did matter, and that their ideas about their child's particular learning needs and preferences would be considered by teachers where practicable.

Chiltern

According to current members of the leadership team it has been a four-year journey from a handful of piecemeal parent partnership activities being offered to the current situation, with a firm commitment in this area from the executive headteacher, the head of school, a member of the leadership team who has responsibility for parental engagement and a small team of key personnel who deliver a variety of coherent initiatives. The informal audit that was carried out on Kath's arrival, combined with a conscious effort on the part of the newly-formed leadership group to discover from parents and staff what they thought was needed, led to rapid improvements in provision. Another important factor was knowing what the school had the capacity to offer at the time, as well as working out how additional capacity could be developed, whether that was a specific part of the site for the hub, a community garden or an additional member of staff.

The school built on the knowledge about, and understanding of, the parents and the catchment accrued by one early-years teacher as she became an assistant headteacher with responsibility, amongst other things, for parent partnership. As Kath puts it, 'We all agree that our parents absolutely need to be involved in the life of our school', a determination that led at the time to a number of conversations that began with 'What do we do with parents?' The response from staff was typically, 'Could we ...' as they suggested ideas that had long been on their minds or perhaps even tried at small scale on an *ad hoc* basis, to which Kath was eager to reply, 'Absolutely!' The resulting activity clearly stemmed from a wealth of ideas from the school team, combined with Kath's openness for her colleagues to try whatever might work to meet the parents' need to be involved and supported, and consequently for their children to thrive and learn.

The leadership team knows that in the life of a child a holistic approach is needed for learning to happen effectively, so the family around each and every child has to be considered. This means school and home working together to a common purpose, so supportive efforts naturally go beyond supporting the material needs of families into passing on learning-related knowledge and skills to parents wherever possible. For example, to get parents over the threshold into Foundation Stage, staff hold 'Read with Me' sessions fortnightly, where paired reading is modelled and a free book sent home to everyone who attends. There is also a playgroup for children aged children aged nought to three years, attended at times by the school nurse who is available to answer parents' questions about child development, especially that of the brain, especially in what is often referred to as the 'first thousand days' from conception to 24 months. Linked to this notion is another group, 'Bump to Baby', run by the school nurse. Four years ago, 'growth-mindset' meetings were held in the hall as part of initial efforts to share the school's new approach to being positive about every pupil's learning potential. Today, the school has a curriculum statement on its website, as well as a link to the Thrive Trust's comprehensive document which talks about the goal of each human being, from the moment they are conceived, to 'seek sense in the world we experience', and goes in in great detail to explain the part that its schools will seek to play in this process. This includes ways in which children will be encouraged to build subject schemas so that parents can have the information they might need to support the school's educational ambitions.

Brunel

One of the school's strengths is in the use of class blogs to share with parents what the children are learning about in school. They are designed to allow pupils not just to talk to their parents about what they've done in their lessons but also to show them. They include activities completed, key words used and core concepts covered, and more and more parents are accessing them. They also describe ways in which parents can help with their children's learning at home, something that the school realised parents were keen to have.

Every term there is a curriculum web on each class's blog, based on the umbrella theme for the term and the knowledge and skills to be acquired. This is then followed by weekly updates from the class teacher, consisting of text, photographs, and sometimes a link to a video, all showing what the class has covered and how the pupils are generally progressing towards the curriculum intent. Big gaps emerged for some children during the COVID-19 lockdowns of 2020 and 2021, so Mini Maths has been adopted as a programme throughout the school, and the idea of KIRFs (Key Instant Recall Facts) has been implemented so that parents are clear about what they can do to help build up their child's mathematical knowledge. The blogs contain links to free online games to play and other informative websites to visit which children are encouraged to point out to their parents when they get home. When posted on the class blog, the running commentary on how an area of maths such as fractions is developing provides possible next steps for children to explore at home, and the school is experimenting with virtual meetings at the end of term so that parents can get together if they wish to discuss how they and their children have found the learning during that time. This is also an opportunity for teachers to show how they have approached teaching the KIRFs in school. This latest practice arose during the lockdowns, when many parents were supporting their children's learning during the school day, and staff are looking at ways to maintain what has proven to be a popular development.

As part of its thrust on teaching phonics Brunel has adopted Read Write Inc., and teachers email to all parents a link to a video of the latest sound so that they can support their child's learning of it effectively. There is also a library of maths games that can be borrowed, once again based on informal research showing that this was previously an area where parents didn't feel equipped to help with learning. Policies associated with learning, such as that covering the school's approach to calculation, are regularly sent home so that parents are aware of how learning tasks are tackled in school and to minimise children's confusion where possible. The school has a relatively large number of pupils with ASD (autism spectrum disorder), so a champion has been appointed to work specifically with them and their families. All of these efforts are intended to encourage parents to see themselves as very much involved in their child's schooling and wider education, should they choose to do so.

The school takes mental health and wellbeing very seriously, and a recent audit identified the need for a leader in this area, so Paul is undertaking modular training with the Carnegie Centre of Excellence to equip him for this crucial role. The school also has three mental health champions, each of whom has responsibility for one part of the school community – pupils, parents and staff. The first two ensure that the school is providing appropriate support and signposting for children and their parents in this area of their lives, whilst also aiming to provide a coherent, family-based approach when this is desirable.

Carrington

During the pandemic lockdowns, the vast majority of parents 'gave it their best shot', as headteacher Kate puts it, given that they had little or no training in supporting formal learning activities, and were often trying to fit in 'working from home' at the same time. Kate and the other members of the senior leadership team kept in touch with those vulnerable children who were at home, whilst they and other staff taught key workers' children and the most vulnerable who were able to come into the school throughout the various lockdowns. Throughout this challenging period staff drew on and developed their knowledge of the parent community, and Kate began to audit informally the processes in place for parental involvement and engagement so that she and the SLT would be well-placed to develop what she sees as a key area of school life. As a new leader she soon had a clear idea of how she wanted things to be, without committing her intentions to a formal written policy but preferring to let practice develop organically and speak for itself.

In respect of the curriculum the school shares with parents a core Reading Spine of suggested books that can help create a living library in their minds. There is also a related vocabulary spine, available to parents, through which their children can assemble a bank of words to use in their own talking and writing. Much of the information that parents need if they are to support their children with those learning conversations that the research suggests are the most effective, comes through Tapestry (early years) and ClassDojo (Key Stage 1), as with other schools included in my visits and conversations for this book. At Carrington teachers are expected to post something for each class three times a week, in a virtual space private to their class, to which parents can respond with a comment if they wish. Each child has a portfolio that parents can also add work into, sometimes in response to the home-learning challenges that have been set by the school but also spontaneously from the child's personal activities and interests, such as with one Year 1 girl who had been involved in a local drama group. In this instance Kate saw the post and commented with 'This is brilliant. Can she show it in assembly, please?' After consultation with her parents this was duly done, providing an excellent example of the power of the parent-school interface to foster engagement.

Of course, not all parents are as receptive to such opportunities as the school would like them to be. As Kate puts it, 'Therein lies the challenge', but she and her team are determined to continue to use all the means possible to share as widely, and safely, what the children are doing in school. One recent example from Year 1 is the photographs shared in ClassDojo of the wide variety of containers that the children discovered around school as part of their work on capacity. Year 2 carried out a traffic survey, the results of which also made it onto the ClassDojo pages. Another frequent photographic subject shared with parents in this way is the Forest School programme that has become a vital part of Carrington's educational offer. The visibility of all three members of the SLT is enhanced by the fact that they can also post directly into the Tapestry and ClassDojo systems so that they become 'virtually' ever-present in the learning that is taking place across the school, and thus more knowledgeable about what is actually being taught and what is coming back from children and parents in response.

Another communication forum for the school is its open Facebook page, curated solely by Kate but frequently and engagingly posted onto in spite of other demands on her time. It's clearly a priority, providing information for anyone in the local community, especially prospective parents, but also a showcase that allows everyone connected to the school to feel the sense of pride and belonging that valued organisations like schools tend to thrive on. Weekly, eye-catching and informative newsletters are also sent out digitally to parents, as well as being retrospectively available on the website.

In spite of all that the school hopes for from parents as partners, Kate isn't complacent about the degree to which the whole parent body is able, or chooses, to buy into her expectations. She recognises that 'We can fill those cups up to overflowing with things we'd like them to do, but if they're not happening then it's not going to work'. This understanding reflects my own view that a school's knowledge about uptake is an essential part of any parental involvement and engagement strategy, and so monitoring of all the communication systems used becomes an essential part of good practice, as well as the openness to parental inputs about improvement demonstrated by so much of what Carrington espouses.

Littlecoates

Vice Principal Emma, who joined the school in September 2021, already knows the community well enough to state that 'we have to work harder with some of our parents because maybe they don't value schooling as much as we would like'. She suggests that such parents possibly think 'We've not done it, so it's not important to us'. A typical comment about their child's progress at parents' evening might be 'I was never any good at maths, so I don't think they'll get it'. She goes on to say that if parents aren't confident with a piece of learning it's easier not to do, or even look at, it with their child, rather than showing that they aren't capable themselves.

She was responsible for introducing ClassDojo to the school on her arrival, co-ordinating and overseeing a trial in three classes during the Autumn term, before rolling it out to the whole school, from Reception to Year 6, in the spring, having ironed out any wrinkles. As a way of engaging with all parents it's proved a huge success, with excellent uptake during the trial period that has since been replicated more widely. Those parents who don't feel confident enough to come in and see the teacher, or use the phone to get in touch, have taken readily to the informality of ClassDojo's communication processes. It's possible to use 'text speak' which helps less-literate parents and those who speak English as an additional language, with the translate facility being available as messages are received and sent, and with the enabling parental perception from texting that school staff are much less likely to make judgements about their spelling or grammar in this medium. The system is also private within the class or school, so parents are generally very happy for their children to be involved, as are wider family members like grandparents, who often have responsibility for pupils before and after the school day. Another advantage is that ClassDojo is free for school and parents, although add-ons can be bought for the children if their parents wish.

In terms of knowing the extent of parental participation and, by implication, the degree to which parents are involved and engaged more widely at home in their children's learning, the school's principal, Neville, and Emma can both see who has been accessing the ClassDojo provision and then take steps to encourage those who haven't to participate. Currently, the school has nearly 100 percent uptake in all classes. If a particular message hasn't been read

Figure 6.1 A ClassDojo mobile phone screen at Littlecoates

the school can follow up with a letter, a phone call or by someone catching the parent at the gate for a quick word. The efficiency and effectiveness of two-way communication throughout the school has greatly improved since the system was adopted.

The school's knowledge of the parent community is massively informed by the interactions of the nursery teacher Annette (also the early years manager) and her team, with children's parents on intake. As with most schools, home visits are carried out before the children start at Littlecoates, and various workshops or 'clinics' are regularly delivered by staff, and external partners, on such subjects as behaviour, phonics and reading. One of the benefits of the ClassDojo package is that parents readily know what their child has been learning about in school on a given day. This means that when a teacher posts a picture of a child mixing paint, for example, by that evening when the parent sits down to look at the image with their child it's immediately possible for a conversation to begin about what is going on, how the child feels about it and what they think they've learnt.

Beaumont Hill

Following an Ofsted inspection in 2017 that described the academy as 'inadequate', parent voice was one aspect of school life that was identified as needing some expansion, so there was a clear driver for school staff to develop this aspect of its provision quickly. As part of a wide and thorough consultation on parent voice and engagement a group of parents looked with school leaders at communication systems that were in use in other schools and selected Frog as being the package that they felt would suit Beaumont Hill best, with Tapestry chosen for early years. The expectations for staff and parent involvement in the use of Frog are the same across the school, and ClassDojo is also used purely as a behaviour-management system with those primary children for whom it is appropriate. For many of the pupils immediate and concrete rewards and affirmations, such as high-fives and stickers, are more suited to helping them with their self-regulation, but parents are kept informed about their children's behaviour whichever system is being used to help them to manage it.

With all of the children having an EHCP (Education Health and Care Plan), which may contain some very sensitive personal information, there is the need for high levels of confidentiality, and the Frog system meets the Trust's GDPR (General Data Protection Regulation) criteria. Each family has its own Frog pupil page, which only they can see, it being an in-house-only system. This page contains pictures of the work they've done in school, photographs and video clips of them carrying out activities (if permission has been given by the parents) and whole-school or class written communications, such as educational visit letters. The class teacher will also add a daily comment about the pupil's achievements and attitude which will be bespoke to the child according to what parents have asked to have included. For the more academically able pupils it's about what they've done that day in educational terms, as well as how they've been supported in their learning, whereas for those with more profound or complex needs parents might want to know what their food intake has been, how many times they've been toileted or how their hydrotherapy session went. In this respect, the staff's knowledge of each family is clearly crucial. All communication between school and home is niche to the particular learning pathway that the child is on.

Helen explains that she applied specifically for the assistant headteacher role that included responsibility for 'parental engagement' as it is referred to at Beaumont Hill, as she is passionate about this area of the school's work and believes that she can make an impact in it. During the pandemic, parents were talking to staff in school during online learning to identify their children's physical and emotional needs that needed support, so lots of social stories were taken out to homes to explain why they had to be at home to avoid catching COVID-19 and why their teachers were appearing on screen. Children with ASD (autism spectrum disorder) found the screen time easier in some ways because they were inclined to be less distracted by the pressure of sitting in a classroom and coping with social norms.

Head of early years and the primary phase, Kirsty, describes work the school did prior to the pandemic to provide in-house training for parents, using a questionnaire that was sent home with tick boxes based on what staff thought parents might need, plus an open suggestion box at the end. When the responses were analysed Kirsty discovered that most parents found sensory regulation, intensive interactions and teaching children to read at the pre-phonics stage the most popular with parents, so the training offer was designed around offering what they had asked for. Unfortunately, it was difficult to deliver parent training during the lockdowns because during the day most of the parents were trying to support their child's learning, and after school they were still committed to their carer role, as well as staff workload being an issue. However, now that COVID-19 infection rates and severity are diminishing Helen and Kirsty are both looking forward to getting the in-house training

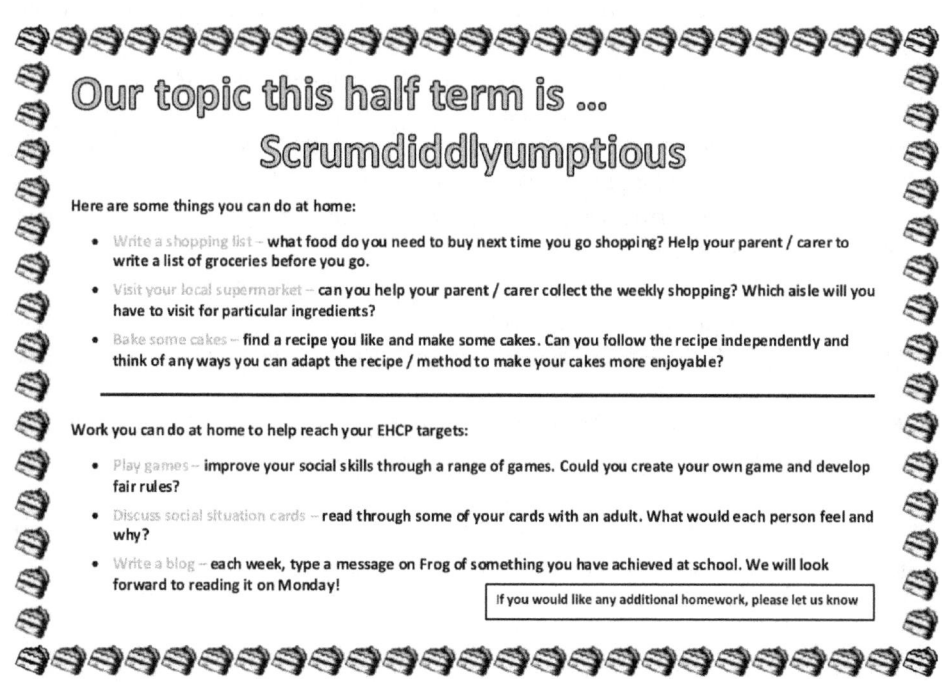

Figure 6.2 A typical Beaumont Hill topic plan

programme for parents of primary children up and running again. Almost certainly, another questionnaire will also be going out soon to see what the priorities of the current crop of parents might be.

Key ideas in this chapter

When reflecting on the six accounts above I have tried to pick out some of the actions and approaches that appear to have fostered mutual knowledge in the parent-school interface most effectively. Some of them have been put forward by more than one of the schools chosen. As with other chapters there is space at the bottom of the list for you to add your own observations. You may also like to look back at the suggested model in Chapter 2 to see if any of them can be mapped onto the diagram that I have shared.

- Thoroughly and honestly audit and evaluate the school's parent partnership policies, practices and procedures.
- Determine the school's current capacity to deliver high-quality parent partnership and identify ways in which this might be increased if necessary.
- Develop a deep knowledge and understanding of the local community.
- Use evidence-informed approaches in teaching and learning, sharing the rationale with parents and the wider community.
- Operate an open-door policy to encourage parents to share their aspirations and views.
- Be prepared to meet parents off-site if it helps them to engage in dialogue.
- Use family workshops to share with parents the school's approach to teaching and learning.
- Encourage staff, including leaders, to demonstrate to parents how well they know and understand the children that they serve.
- Seek widely throughout the school community for ideas that might be adopted.
- Engage with parents before their children reach school age if possible.
- Empower parents as partners in their child's learning and development by sharing information about how this process typically takes place.
- Share with parents, by the easiest possible means, what is happening in classrooms to encourage conversations at home about learning.
- Take mental health and emotional wellbeing seriously throughout the school, including that of parents.
- Adopt an electronic platform to allow safe, informative and accessible two-way sharing of learning experiences and outcomes at home and in school.
- Constantly evaluate the effectiveness of the school's parent partnership offer.
- Provide in-house training for parents in specific areas of interest such as ASD, using staff expertise where possible to develop ongoing working relationships and two-way sharing of knowledge and understanding.

Knowledge 73

You might like to add your own key ideas here from your reading in this chapter and any further thoughts about earlier material:

Conversation starters

Here are some follow-up questions to help you develop your own thinking about the ideas that I've proposed, and any others that have been important to you in relation to securing effective parent partnership as widely as possible.

- In what ways do I as a practitioner, and we as a school, get to know our parents as a group and individually where appropriate?
- How do we encourage parents to get to know the school's staff, systems and processes for themselves, enabling them to be comfortable about engaging with us and their child's schooling, wider education and learning?
- How might we improve these, based on the ideas and examples shared in this chapter and a wider reading of this book and other sources?

7 Understanding and empathy

Ways in which each school's staff demonstrate that they listen to what is really being said, share their own related experiences appropriately and empower parents to take ownership of their strengths and areas for growth

Rathfern

A number of staff with primary-age children live in the local community, and many of them have similar lived experiences to those of the parents that the school serves. This sometimes allows them to understand the circumstances faced by parents and to empathise accurately with the challenges faced, or the opportunities offered, in their part of Lewisham, and further afield in London. These staff are also able to be advocates for parents when their colleagues are trying to put themselves in the shoes of others.

Deeper understanding and empathy are instrumental in helping parents to see Rathfern as a safe place, a view which is taken on by their children in turn, although in some cases this operates the other way round staff tell me, with children providing a lead to their parents. The school avoids describing parents as 'hard to reach', preferring if anything the term 'hard to hear', a phrase which drives staff to try even harder to allow parent voice to reach them by whatever means are available. Staff work very hard on not judging, an aspiration that in my view relies heavily on empathising effectively. The school embraces parents for who they are and celebrates them as much as possible. This entails taking the trouble to understand their abilities, skills, hopes and aspirations and valuing them privately or publicly whenever they align with the school's moral purpose.

For a number of years the school had 'Chatter Matters' in place to encourage early language development in its youngest children, having picked up that this was an area that parents wanted some support with. As the research shows, home conversation is massively important to children's educational outcomes, so this was clearly a desirable intervention. Since then, other initiatives have included weekly opportunities, every Friday, for parents to share this key skill with their children in school. Recognising that a lot of parents were unsure about safe internet use for their children, the school put on an IT clinic where parents could bring along their equipment for free advice, followed by an e-safety training event. The opportunity to get practical support beforehand was instrumental in increasing attendance substantially in comparison to earlier efforts to engage with parents in this area of safeguarding. Another example of understanding and empathy has been in the nature of the phonics workshops offered to Year 1 parents, where current techniques are demonstrated in ways that recognise how much the teaching of sounds in learning to read has changed over time, compared to the methods that many parents encountered when they were learning. Those parents who have recently arrived in the country, and for whom English is a second language, clearly have their own issues in relation to phonics, and staff are equally skilled in identifying these and offering the support necessary during the workshops offered.

The various lockdowns in place during the COVID-19 pandemic allowed parents to understand more completely their own children's specific learning needs better, as they worked alongside them on learning activities set by the school, and many who had children on the SEND register became more communicative about them. The school will take this new awareness forward over the next few years with the parents concerned and is keen to find ways in which this effect can be harnessed in the future, perhaps by using blended virtual and face-to-face workshops periodically, as had been the case pre-COVID, although to a lesser extent than became the case during the long periods of enforced home learning experienced by many children at that time.

An area of parent partnership has traditionally been that of parenting skills, and one member of staff at Rathfern is trained to deliver the Triple P programme, central to which is the process by which parents are able to openly and honestly describe their own parenting experiences, explain what difficulties they might be having at home, and then to explore how to have tricky conversations with their children, and to begin to set some supported targets for improvement. Before COVID, the programme has involved some group meetings, with participants providing traditional dishes to be shared by everyone. Children have sometimes been present on such occasions, and the school is about to reintroduce the scheme as the pandemic subsides, knowing how much of an impact it has had on a number of families, and consequently on their children's learning outcomes.

The school has a pastoral 'Unlocking Potential' team in place, with its manager offering wellbeing and mental health support to pupils, and advice to parents in this crucial area, including weekly tips in the school's newsletter.

Chiltern

Head of School Jacqui and her leadership team recognised that holding the school's regular coffee mornings in the school meant that parents would have to come past the school office to get there, which was a 'no-no' for many of them back in the early days of her headship. Unfortunately, this meant that these parents just wouldn't feel comfortable about coming to events that had been arranged. This realisation led to the creation of the community hub, the use of which has already been described in the previous chapter. The room chosen was already part of the site, a prefabricated building close to the main entrance, and it soon proved to be the perfect halfway-house between the local community and the school building itself. Many more parents were prepared to come into the hub, and it was only a short walk from the school so that key staff involved in parent outreach activities could easily access it.

Designing parent communication systems has been another key area of the school's parent partnership work, relying heavily on empathy and understanding in relation to parents' circumstances, their reading skills and the availability of devices like mobile phones and tablets. Initially, when Jacqui and her colleagues were trying to get the word out about their plans, parents were bombarded with fliers, text messages and newsletters, in order to establish the hub. Now, a text message every Thursday is sufficient to remind people of the hub's existence and to whet their appetite for what is on offer this week. At the end of the pandemic one mum was feeling a bit down, so one of the staff invited her to get involved in the newly-created community garden which has really helped. As she said once she had taken the courageous step to participate, 'It's just nice to have a purpose again'. COVID-19 has been every isolating for many parents, and the hub has quickly become the highlight of the week for many. I was fortunate to be able to experience the hub first-hand, during a cookery session, and it came across as a safe and nurturing space for all those parents who attended. The additional funding that was secured for the community garden has provided another valuable opportunity because many of the school's families don't have a back garden, being limited instead to quite a small yard in the vast majority of cases.

The school thinks of the parents and wider family as the support team for each child, so helping to maintain their mental health and wellbeing is a high priority, with working in the community garden beginning to have a very positive impact on this aspect of the life of the increasing numbers of parents joining in with growing plants and developing the hard landscaping of the project.

It's been proven that reading with children can be an excellent way of fostering a love of books and also developing key knowledge and skills associated with the reading process, but with some single parents trying to get round five or six children in an evening teachers and support staff try hard to be understanding about how much capacity there is for each child to be heard every night, as might be the expectation. As Jacqui says, 'We need to work out how to get parents to help us without putting too much strain on them'. This empathetic approach clearly seeks to get the balance right so that parents enjoy as much as possible the time they spend supporting their children's work and discussing it with them. This should ensure that, as time goes on, the vast majority of parents will want to seek out ways to work in partnership with the school, rather than avoiding engagement with what might be seen as irrelevant drudgery.

In order to develop pupils' cultural capacity schools have often tried to encourage their pupils to take up hobbies, but for many Chiltern families the possibility of funding dance classes or rugby league training sessions is not one that they can contemplate. According to Jacqui the parent partnership lead and the pastoral support worker are both expert at not making their offer to temporarily fund such activities seem like charity to the recipient parents. They are both also prepared to show tough love in the challenging things they sometimes have to say to parents in meetings, and in spite of being empathetic and non-judgemental in such circumstances, they are also uncompromising in their expectations of the practical support that they need to see evidence of in the home visits that they regularly undertake as part of their roles.

Brunel

Knowing their families as they do, staff are keen to offer parents' meetings, and other opportunities to interact effectively, in ways and at times that are most convenient and helpful to the parents concerned. As the school emerges from the pandemic parents' consultations are now offered virtually, by telephone or face-to-face, a range of options that allows members of the staff team to offer a much more bespoke service than was previously the case, something that may be one of the few positive legacies of COVID-19.

In dealing with parents Paul agrees that being able to alter his register and vocabulary to suit the situation can help him to build positive relationships with them. He has also found that sharing his own experiences of parenting, in a limited and professional way, has at times helped him to show understanding and empathy with his pupils' parents. A typical comment might be 'Having children of my own I know what it's like'. On a recent occasion one morning at the gate a child was very reluctant to come into school because they had toothpaste and egg all down the front of their jumper. He was soon able to reassure both the child and its parent that 'if that's the problem I can soon find you a clean jumper, so come on in and we'll sort it'. As he says several times during our conversation, 'We know our families pretty well', knowledge which at best leads to a shared understanding and the kind of empathy that readily defuses potentially challenging situations.

The school has had a food bank since the pandemic, serving as it does a relatively deprived area economically, and Paul remembers the staff and volunteers being aware of those families who didn't have a working cooker and who therefore weren't given frozen sausages in their food parcels. Rather, bespoke packages were put together that showed how much trouble had been taken to match what was available to those who needed it. Those organising the food bank allocations were keen to make sure that parents only had to have the conversation about their circumstances once, thereby avoiding the need to keep repeating themselves. Another area where the school can respond to individual need is in the area of wrap-around care, when external agencies are able to make referrals that remove the need for parents to pay for an agreed period, in the case of particular hardship. The school's free breakfast club is in the process of restarting now that COVID-19 finally appears to be on the wane.

One final example from Brunel in this section is the Christmas jumper initiative, whereby the school put out an appeal to parents and staff for spare items that could be sensitively made available to children whose parents didn't have the resource to buy one this year. It could be argued that avoiding the Christmas jumper scenario altogether would have 'poverty-proofed' the children concerned, but I get the impression that the leadership team at Brunel want all pupils to experience everything that is on offer culturally across Britain, and this was one way to alleviate a problem that had been identified. According to Paul about 20 jumpers appeared, were worn for the charitable event and then returned washed for use next year.

Carrington

During the pandemic children who were ill or self-isolating were able to join the school's virtual assemblies, something that was very much appreciated by parents, as they could see how much it meant to their children especially, to be included in a vital method for maintaining a sense of school community for the whole family during challenging and disconnected times for everyone. Since school has returned to something more normal 'Stay and Play' has returned in the early-years classes at Carrington, renewing the opportunities it offers to the staff and parents alike to understand each other as partners around children's learning through play and more formal, directed activity. For those parents new to the school this has been the first opportunity to see and experience the school and its staff first-hand, rather than through photographs, videos and virtual meetings. The school has recently taken on a new scheme for teaching phonics, and workshops for parents have provided another chance to deepen relationships between parents and staff, as well as to pass on the knowledge and skills that should allow the parents to support their children's learning.

Another area that Headteacher Kate was keen to develop when she arrived at Carrington was parents' evening, or parent consultations as she chooses to call them, following successful experiences of this idea in her previous school. More detail about the format will follow in the next chapter, but the decision (as the school emerged from the pandemic) to allow parents some freedom in how they met with their child's teacher to discuss their progress was something that reflected an empathetic approach to the process. Parents were offered virtual or face-to-face meetings, a decision that put greater demands on staff but which put parents' needs at the centre of a process which, after all, should be designed to encourage as many as possible to attend. For those who wished to discuss their child's education in the school this was provided in as COVID-safe a way as possible. For those who would rather meet up virtually, perhaps because of difficulties finding a babysitter, greater efficiency of time in a busy working week, one separated parent living away from the school, for their own mental wellbeing, or for any other perfectly valid reason, this was arranged. The school has an online system for arranging parent-teacher consultations for those who find this helpful, although other options are also available for those who prefer to use them. All of this suggests that the staff at Carrington are making every possible effort to really understand their parents' individual circumstances and then provide conditions in which as many as possible can attend those twice-yearly formal meetings that reinforce the parent-teacher partnership.

Potential barriers to learning related to a child's family circumstances have been even more closely identified by Kate and her deputy, Rachel, during the last year, partly through the local authority engaging Marc Rowlands, a well-respected authority on Pupil Premium, to work with all of its schools. There has been a shift in the mindset of staff which has begun to alter their perspective on the children concerned and their understanding of the challenges faced by some children and their parents, often due to a material, emotional or educational deficit at home. As a result staff at Carrington are increasingly determined to challenge a view that suggests that such challenges cannot be overcome, replacing it with the ambition that all children can succeed in reaching their true educational potential, especially when parents are willing and able to share that aspiration.

Kate is aware that she and other members of the Carrington staff team occasionally find themselves going above and beyond their usual professional commitment, often by understanding a parent's particular characteristics or needs, and intuitively communicating to that parent that they 'get what you're handling' as she puts it. It's one thing to be empathetic of a parents' wants or needs, but I believe it takes that feeling to an even more empowering level when a teacher, teaching assistant, learning mentor or family support worker manages to sensitively communicate this deeper understanding to the person concerned. The resulting rapport can really drive successful educational partnership I've often found.

Understanding and empathy 79

Figure 7.1 The Carrington Stay and Play activity in Reception

Littlecoates

During the COVID-19 lockdowns daily or weekly phone calls were made to parents of those pupils not in school by members of the leadership team, class teachers and other relevant staff, according to the perceived vulnerability of the children concerned. Google Classroom is another system for supporting and encouraging dialogue between parents and staff, which is a legacy of the pandemic. Most of the older pupils in the school still do their homework on this simple and easy-to-use tool, which has the added advantage of linking well with Class-Dojo. It is used by teachers and support staff, especially with older pupils, allowing them to set group tasks for a number of children to collaborate on electronically. Understanding the desirability of using packages familiar to the children to reach out to and engage their parents strikes me as a very empathetic approach, encouraging as it should those learning conversations within families that the research suggests can be supremely effective in improving educational outcomes.

As mentioned briefly in the previous chapter the NSPCC (National Society for the Prevention of Cruelty to Children) is funding a long-term project in the West Marsh area of Grimsby called 'Together for Childhood'. The charity aims to work with local communities to make them safer for children, and the school has two link workers who visit at least weekly so that parents can drop in and see them. Additional activities such as craft events are also provided as part of the project, and the workers are also responsible for running coffee mornings. All of these events are advertised widely in all the formats mentioned so far, and parents relish the opportunity to talk with the workers about a variety of issues, including their children's wellbeing, behaviour and family finances. The school's externally provided mental health practitioners also visit the sessions, as well as the local PCSOs (Police Community Support Officers), so that specialist advice and support can be accessed. The link workers also sit at the back of the hall with invited parents during celebration assemblies so that the parents and pupils get used to seeing them around. The intention of this embedded approach is chiefly to gain trust and to avoid them being seen as figures of authority, or associated with stigma, but rather as a supportive resource. In addition to a universal offer to parents to attend the coffee mornings specific individuals are also invited based on the school's understanding of their particular needs, often identified by the well-resourced pastoral team.

A key member of the staff team is Dawn, Littlecoates's office manager, who is described by Vice Principal Emma as 'the heart and soul of the school', a function of how long she has worked there, her approachability and accessibility and her knowledge of the families. She is also able to empathise with their different circumstances and to share this with them through her friendly, down-to-earth manner. According to Emma, Dawn often becomes a bridge between parent and teacher so that familiarity, openness and honesty are able to develop well enough between the two to allow for more effective communication, and to foster genuine partnership around the child and their attitudes, behaviour and learning.

The school's SENDCo, Kate, is another name that crops up when talking to parents about the school's partnership with them. Once again Emma has an accurate understanding of Kate's place in the parents' affections, describing her as 'no nonsense and no frills', an attitude that parents quickly recognise and generally appreciate she tells me. A typical example might be when Kate has spent considerable time and effort arranging an appointment with another service provider, only for the parent to fail to attend. 'If you're not going to take them to the appointment, don't come and see me' would be her likely response, insisting (as she does) that parents put their child at the centre of their efforts in the same way that she tries to. Emma believes that Littlecoates parents nearly always like that kind of straight talk.

Delivering genuine understanding and empathy can be hugely time and energy consuming, so the two pastoral team members, who split the role during the week, make a significant contribution to the school's effectiveness in this respect by making time to listen to individual parents, and then signpost them to those practitioners, both inside and beyond the school, who might be able to help. One of them joins Neville, the principal, at the school gate at the beginning and end of the day so that parents are able to get hold of them easily. This gateway presence also includes the local PCSOs and the NSPCC link workers periodically so that as many professionals as possible are able to get alongside parents with a listening ear and, wherever possible, an understanding and empathetic response.

Beaumont Hill

Having quite a few children with health conditions, Beaumont Hill stayed working with bubbles during the pandemic longer than most mainstream schools. During that time the pastoral team had to gauge which families were inclined to protect their dignity and, therefore, didn't want to accept help, even though they needed it financially. As the first port of call the pastoral team's members are very empathetic, and so it wasn't broadly known which families had received each form of help available, a consideration that was very much appreciated by the parents concerned, maintaining their dignity as it did.

On a number of occasions Helen, the parental engagement lead, was told by parents that their work commitments were preventing them from attending the parents' forum, so she took their email addresses and now adds them to the Teams meeting invitations so that they can join virtually if they are able, while other parents are gathered face-to-face in the school hall. There is a virtual page where parents can add subjects that they'd like to be discussed at the forum, and then the minutes from each meeting are freely available for any parents to look it if they weren't able to attend, either online or in person. Helen is aware that pupils aren't always aware of the role the forum plays in the life of the school, so she has organised a competition for them to design a logo for the meeting, with parents then choosing a winner from the suggestions received. She feels that this will also serve to raise the profile of the forum, as well as drawing parents' eyes to any future communications about the meetings and outcomes. It will also be featured on the school website. Helen and Kirsty, the early years and primary lead, are also keen to strengthen the links between the parent forum and the student council so that pupils have an opportunity to talk directly to a group of receptive parents about what they've learnt, and about how their parents have helped them.

One recent example of a collaboration between the parents and children was an art carousel where family groups were able to access and enjoy a wide range of creative opportunities together. The work of the forum is a great example of a school listening to its parents and involving them in key decisions about all aspects of school life. It also strikes me as a genuine attempt by key staff to get alongside the parents and 'walk a few steps in their shoes', in ways that should help them to better understand the children's home experience and learning opportunities away from school, as well as the joys and frustrations felt by their parents as they support them in this.

Key ideas in this chapter

When reflecting on the six accounts above I have tried to pick out some of the actions and approaches that appear to have fostered mutual understanding and empathy in the parent-school interface most effectively. Some of them have been put forward by more than one of the schools chosen. As with other chapters there is space at the bottom of the list for you to add your own observations. You may also like to look back at the suggested model in Chapter 2 to see if any of them can be mapped onto the diagram that I have shared.

- Use the knowledge and experiences of local staff to help the whole team to empathise effectively with parents.
- Try replacing 'hard to reach' with 'hard to hear'.
- Use incentives based on an understanding of parents' circumstances to encourage participation in supportive events and activities.
- Harness techniques used in the pandemic to make blended offers in the future.
- Find and adopt a suitable programme to allow staff to get alongside parents in developing their parenting.
- Offer or signpost mental health and wellbeing support to parents.
- Develop a part of the school that is easily accessible to parents and use it for key events, activities and meetings.

- Provide safeguarded opportunities for parents to 'find themselves' and build their self-efficacy and self-esteem.
- Develop sustainable ways for parents to support their child's reading.
- Offer a variety parent-school interface opportunities that are convenient to all parents.
- Make support as bespoke as possible to reflect families' particular needs.
- Create interactive home-school opportunities so that staff and parents can understand each other better over time.
- Find ways to share with parents the nature of the relationship between staff and pupils so that they have a clearer understanding of the dynamics that might foster effective learning.
- Encourage staff in a range of roles to share their own experiences of parenting carefully so that they can demonstrate empathy with parents who are dealing with a variety of situations and circumstances.
- Work sensitively with partner organisations to deliver a wider range of services at a deeper level than the school's own capacity.
- Show sensitivity to parents' feelings of dignity when offering them support.

You might like to add your own key ideas here from your reading in this chapter and any further thoughts about earlier material:

Conversation starters

Here are some follow-up questions to help you develop your own thinking about the ideas that I've proposed and any others that have been important to you in relation to securing effective parent partnership as widely as possible.

- In what ways do I as a practitioner, and we as a school, make the effort to really understand the experiences of, and circumstances faced by, parents, and to demonstrate to them any empathy felt?
- How do we encourage parents to get to know the school and its staff well enough to understand, and empathise with, the challenges and demands that we face in trying to educate their child?
- How might we improve these, based on the ideas and examples shared in this chapter and a wider reading of this book and other sources?

8 Relationship

The links and bonds that are created between the school and its parents, leading to clear communication, thoughtful responses to ideas and shared decision making

Rathfern

One of the purposes that Rathfern sets itself is the breaking down of barriers to educational success, and effective relationships are at the heart of this ambition. Where they are necessary, safeguarding conversations are not shied away from but are used as a platform to offer families further support. Incidents or circumstances are used as an opportunity for staff with a good relationship with parents to ask, 'What can we do?' The conversations that ensue may lead to an agreed early help referral, for example, so that support can be quickly put in place for vulnerable families, in partnership with school staff.

The intention in such instances is to be 'clear but kind', as one member of staff put it, because emotionally holding the parent will almost always have a positive influence on the child and their learning. Visibility of key staff is a key part of the way that Rathfern develops a sense of relationship, for instance by being present and available on the playground at the start and end of the school day. A number of events have been offered that draw on and cement the links that develop through this constant presence, such as 'bringing up a family on a fiver'. The Friends of Rathfern group has also been instrumental in fostering relationships between parents, as well as those with the school team, through trips to the local park and other activities. The recreational common of Blackheath is described by one member of staff as being 'a stone's throw away', and yet some families appear not to have had the resources, the imagination or the organisational skills to experience what for many is a straightforward venture, such as flying a kite, until the 'friends' group has arranged and delivered it.

As mentioned in Chapter 6 the use of virtual meetings between school staff and parents during the 2020 COVID-19 pandemic was widespread, especially around children's additional needs, which deepened the quality of relationships in ways that have remained for many since the return to pre-pandemic working methods. Of course, face-to-face meetings continued where necessary, under COVID-19 regulations, following government guidelines, and even meeting outdoors where appropriate. Teachers also found the time to make weekly phone calls to the parents of vulnerable children, with this approach being kept where helpful and where staff workload permits. The intention of the school in these interactions has been to foster the 'tough love' approach that underpins so much of its parental engagement work. The use of virtual meetings has also allowed staff to reach more parents than before, especially those who had previously found visiting school a daunting prospect.

One member of staff feels that for some parents school *is* their community, providing such a strong sense of belonging that they are prepared to travel with their child for up to an hour to the school, having moved house to outer London. Having said that, recognising the importance of stability in a child's life has frequently led to the school writing supportive letters to local authorities, making a case for families to be rehoused close to the school.

Chiltern

Staff responsible for delivering parent partnership are very clear that word-of-mouth plays a crucial part in spreading information about what's on offer in the community hub and a range of other initiatives that are designed to enable them to support their child's learning. The use of positive relationships between staff and parents to create this communication network has been at the heart of the last four years of progress in what is seen as a vital aspect of the school's work. Jacqui, head of school, points to other significant relationships with local organisations that have been harnessed to engage with parents, including visits by staff to the family breakfast club hosted by a local Methodist church. They model reading with young children and signpost parents to other services at the club, as well as publicising the school's own activities. When a group of refugees arrived in the area school staff introduced them to the club, and other isolated parents have been taken to local crafting organisations to enable them to develop their social capital. Such efforts by the school recognise the importance for parents of building and maintaining those supportive networks that are desirable if they are to contribute fully to their child's learning. The 'living newspaper' for HU3 is another relatively new local initiative that the school has cultivated links with and written articles for. Executive Headteacher Kath hopes that this will go on to provide another opportunity to portray the school as an essential and relevant part of its community.

Staff are aware of the possibility that all of these efforts to build relationships and provide help might lead to a dependency culture amongst parents. They point to practices such as the 'wellness action plans' that are written jointly by the school, the parent and, where appropriate, the child. The spirit of these agreements is to say to the parents, 'We'll help you, you'll help your child, and they'll take some responsibility too'. One parent recently said, 'I could have one of those too', a suggestion that the school was more than happy to go along with. This is an area that hopefully other parents will be interested in developing for their own benefit and consequently for their children's sake too.

Staff are dotted around the school building and site at the beginning and end of the day so that they are as accessible as possible. The one-way system, introduced when the school reopened as COVID-19 restrictions eased, has been retained as it encourages smooth flow of parents and children, thus also facilitating more effective communication. One member of staff suggested that the result of this availability leads to parents having 'normal conversations with normal people', rather than something more daunting and unwelcoming, such as the brief exchanges with understandably busy and therefore preoccupied teachers that can often be the alternative at drop-off and pick-up. There is a conscious effort to make the whole school a warmer and more welcoming environment for parents, all of which fosters the sense of partnership around children's learning.

The experience of witnessing online lessons live in their homes during the various lockdowns and periods of COVID-related isolation has led a number of parents to say to teachers and support staff, 'I couldn't do your job'. Having said this many have also become much more aware of the way in which their children learn at school, through supporting them in carrying out the tasks that they've been set. Communication about learning has also been improved in the last two years, in ways that Kath and the rest of the school team are keen to continue if appropriate methods can be developed.

Chiltern leaders and staff recognise the importance of fostering strong, empowering relationships between parents. For example, at a recent Chat and Choose session, the school's sensitively run food bank and parent outreach event, a mum who'd had just had another baby was talking about the difficulties she was experiencing in getting on top of her housework. Within days a group of mums had spontaneously gone round to help her to tackle the issues that were getting her down, and she was reportedly soon able to stand on her own two feet with her parenting of the new baby and her older children.

One thing that I observe in the key staff members of the Chiltern team are their communication skills when working with the parents. They come across as very authentic, with a direct style and an engaging, distinctive Hull accent that appears to facilitate the perception of approachability and cultural similarity for many local parents, without them coming across as patronising. Both Jacqui, head of school, and Claire, assistant headteacher, previously worked in the early years phase at Chiltern, and they recognise that this has given them a particularly close relationship with many of the parents. Inevitably, this special link will gradually be eroded as the youngest child in each family makes the transition to secondary school. Therefore, plans are in place to ensure that the current teaching team in the nursery and Foundation Stage are able to pass on by association their own special relationships with parents who are new to the school.

In researching this book, and having time to focus on the issues raised during my conversations with colleagues, I've been struck by the value that is rightly placed on home visits by early years staff when children begin their schooling journey, but I haven't yet met a primary school that accords the same worth to making a courtesy call on parents at home when older children join midterm. Maybe this is something that schools could experiment with, to see what benefits there might be in relationship building.

The assistant headteacher, Claire, in her SENCo role, holds regular 'Together over Tea' drop-in sessions for parents of children with additional needs and disabilities. The half-termly afternoon shared meal sessions for all parents also provide an opportunity for a small group to cook together, under the guidance of a trained member of staff, before taking the food through to the hall where other families join them, followed by craft opportunities for all. In the times of economic hardship prevalent at the time of writing, being able to meet in a warm space and feed the family for free gives parents a real boost, and the opportunities to get to know other parents help to develop a sense of belonging to the school, and provide a chance to buy into the creative, co-operative Chiltern ethos.

Brunel

As I have already explained, relationships between staff and parents often begin, as in many schools, with a wave and a smile at the school gate or with catching someone's eye in passing. However, considerable time and thought are put into building on this initial opening, with systems that now include ClassDojo, whereby good news about learning and other achievements can be readily shared with parents. The system is currently being trialled in Key Stage 1, with a view to rolling it out more widely if it's successful.

In terms of home-school communication staff have found that their experiences during the pandemic have made parents much more likely to access staff emails, partly because the addresses are more accessible as a result of children working at home during lockdowns, but also perhaps because parents have consequently become used to having more direct and regular contact with teachers about learning and other important issues. According to Assistant Head Paul, who also has a considerable teaching commitment, hardly a day goes by when he doesn't get an email from the parent of a child in his class. He finds that these messages are hardly ever 'moans' but usually begin with words like 'Can you just check …' or 'Would you mind if …'. The sense in which they are sent is generally a polite request for help which, if responded to swiftly, really does build up relationship effectively and provides information about the child and their family that is helpful to Paul and his teaching and learning team in class. When children are ill some parents don't just inform the office but also Paul as class teacher, which is something that he has come to appreciate, possibly because it reminds him of his pupils' humanity. For example, he is able to respond efficiently with commiserations and to ask if there's anything he can do to help. The system that has evolved from the initial lockdowns doesn't appear to have become overwhelming in Paul's case and seems to have replaced a lot of the informal chat that used to occur during drop-off and pick-up before COVID-19 precautions came into effect. As Paul sees it, an extra link between home and school has been made by these simple and straightforward communications.

The local authority Education Welfare Officer (EWO), purchased on behalf of the school by the Trust, is another key member of Brunel's parent partnership team. Some parents have had their confidence dented or their habits disrupted by the pandemic, but the sensitive and assertive approach taken to attendance has begun to bear fruit. The school's attendance policy is very clear and concise about what the school will do to encourage good attendance, including detail about rewards for good and improving attendance. It also explains what is expected of parents as they play their part in ensuring that their child is in school for as much of the time as possible. The way in which this policy operates is always based on developing good relationships, with any subsequent joint efforts between home and school hopefully fostering the deepening of these links, and their impact, over time.

Engaging parents directly in their children's learning by devising interesting and informative shared activities has been an effective method for Brunel, especially in recent years. One successful home project has been for everyone to make a model of an Egyptian mummy, bring it into school to be part of a display and receive a certificate for doing so. Using a joint endeavour to build relationships within and beyond the family also generates great opportunities for the kind of conversation that we know is at the heart of successful parental involvement in pupil learning. Another example of shared learning was a very powerful day that saw the children experiencing some fascinating science demonstrations about food from the Royal Institution in the morning, with a group of about 35 parents receiving the same input in the afternoon. There is every chance that there were some fascinating after-school conversations within the families concerned.

Perhaps one of the strongest examples of the school's parent engagement and involvement is its Brunel Friends Association group, with a public page that reveals the group's wider remit than just fundraising for the school, as important as that is. The messages that can be found there include keeping statutory testing in perspective, affordable ideas for family activities in the school holidays and links to local organisations for children, such as the St John's Ambulance Badgers sett, which is located nearby. As Paul explains, there is also an associated closed Facebook group called 'Whoops I forgot to tell you' which is administered and overseen entirely by parents so that all parents can check a variety of minutiae, such as the day of the week when Year 3 wears PE kit or the date of the next parents' evening. The sense of belonging that all of this is able to provide for parents, especially when they have recently joined the school, is a key factor in building a complex and supportive web of relationships that contributes to meeting families' needs and fostering great learning.

When children start a new class at Brunel their parents have emailed to them an introductory profile entitled 'Meet the Teacher' which goes beyond mundane and obvious facts about each person in attempting to reveal something about what makes them really tick. The intention of this open and honest approach is to encourage the recipients to reach out for support or engage in dialogue if they wish. Early career teachers are specifically supported with aspects of relationship building, for example by a staff mentor encouraging one of them to approach a parent when they were having issues with one pupil's behaviour, coaching them on how to make the first move and suggesting what they might say by way of a positive

Figure 8.1 A Brunel parent looks through pre-owned uniforms

introduction. It's not necessarily easy for a 21-year-old teacher to approach a defensive parent of 35 years, but once a positive relationship has been built the paired approach to helping the child to change their behaviours, and perhaps even their education self-schema (see the model in Figure 2.6), has been seen to work well.

On the subject of children with SEND, and with COVID-19 very much in mind, Ofsted observed the following during a recent remote monitoring inspection:

> You maintain strong relationships with the families of pupils with SEND and monitor both their engagement and progress closely. You are working with families to encourage all those pupils who are able to attend school to do so in the current circumstances.

This constitutes a clear external endorsement of what my own visits to the school as a consultant over some years, and my recent conversations with staff and parents in preparation for writing this book, have told me about how important the 'relationship' factor is in Brunel's commitment to genuine parent partnership.

Carrington

A large part of any school's interaction with parents about their child's learning takes place two or three times annually during what used to be called parents' evenings at Carrington but, thanks to Headteacher Kate, are now called parent consultations, based on a title that she used at her previous school in Qatar. When she arrived at the school during the pandemic these meetings had moved online for health and safety reasons, but now that face-to-face get-togethers have been reinstated she encourages staff to include children in the sessions. It makes little sense to Kate to have a child sitting outside a room while two or three adults talk about their educational progress inside. She believes that children love talking about what they can do at school and showing their parents what they've achieved, so in parent consultations as she envisages them the child has an opportunity to talk in some detail about their own learning in ways that I imagine will serve well to reinforce their *education self-schema*, a concept that you may remember Desforges and Abouchaar used in the model cited in Chapter 2. Of course, the consultations are an opportunity for parent-teacher conversations as well, and arrangements can always be made for anything that needs to be said by either party without the child present, for whatever reason, on another occasion and through a variety of media.

In addition to the Class Parent sessions already described in Chapter 5, Kate is committed to building up her own relationship with parents as a 'headteacher at the gate', as she believes that there is no better way to gel the school's parent community. She feels that it's vital not to underestimate the power of standing at the start and end of the school day chatting to everybody and demonstrating that she knows all the children's names. A parent at the on-site pre-school, which isn't run by Carrington, recently came up to Kate and said how impressed she was by her visibility as a headteacher. The mum, also a school leader it transpired, said almost in amazement, 'You're just always visible'. My own conversations with Kate have revealed someone who understands that relationships with parents, whatever the staff member's role in the school, depend for their development on accessibility, approachability and acceptance, all three of which are demonstrated by her devotion to being at the school gate whenever possible.

As part of her commitment to relationship building Kate has further developed links with the nearby junior school to which the vast majority of Carrington's pupils transfer at age seven. She sees as crucial the need for a smooth transition at this age and knows that parents appreciate everything that Carrington can do to prepare their children for the subtle changes that will take place in schooling at Key Stage 2, especially if they have special educational needs or disabilities.

According to Kate relationship exists within expectation – 'Parents expect something from us, and we expect something from them in return. It's not a one-way street'. She goes on to suggest that the children who thrive in school have parents who understand that it's a two-way street. As she puts it: 'They get that the working at home and the reading are part of the success of their child'. And where this isn't yet the case Kate and her staff are clearly passionate about encouraging that understanding in parents. The two-way street is an important concept for her, exemplified anecdotally from her own career by a number of significant occasions when parents have shared with her their deep knowledge and understanding of their child's particular condition, something that she has openly embraced where it has allowed her, and those around her, to teach them more effectively. Kate believes that such openness and honesty are conducive to effective relationships with parents, putting as they do the child's achievements, rather than professional distance or superiority, at the heart of interactions about learning. There are times, too, when it appears as though parents feel entitled to tell teachers how to do their job in ways that they would perhaps hesitate to with other professionals, but on these occasions it should be possible to gently explain the reasons why certain methods are being used, and the thinking behind them.

Littlecoates

The school's principal, Neville, suggests that 'building good relations through communication is a key part of our ethos of partnership', a view that is borne out by the variety of methods that staff use to inform, persuade and reach out to parents. There is also a clear commitment to try something different if one of these processes hasn't worked with a particular family and to keep on trying until a response is received. Neville describes an open-door policy, with easy access to practitioners at senior levels, although health and safety are naturally also important considerations in keeping children, staff and volunteers secure.

The innovative adoption of ClassDojo at Littlecoates, already covered in previous chapters and with other schools, was primarily as a communication tool designed to build school-parent relationships and to foster greater parent involvement and engagement with in-school and at-home learning, whereas other schools have often chosen this and other systems chiefly to reinforce good behaviours for learning in their pupil population. The 'school story' and 'class stories' that lie at the heart of the system are well-visited by parents, with one message pointed out by Emma, the Vice Principal, being viewed within a few days by 32 parents in her class of 28 children. She values her ability to share mindful videos and quotes, not only with her pupils but also with the parents who are able to access the class story, and she often includes parents in debates or polls that she's running with her class, as she firmly believes that this stimulates conversation at home after the end of the school day. As she puts it ClassDojo provides 'a direct link to the classroom'.

A further benefit of the ClassDojo tool is the ease with which parents now get in touch with the school, securely sending messages, photographs (for instance, as evidence of participation in reading for pleasure and extreme reading challenges) to their child's class teacher, and there are also mechanisms for directly contacting teaching assistants, members of the pastoral team and school leaders. Above all, Emma values the potential for efficiently sending positive messages to parents about their children's learning and behaviour. She sees affirmation of parents as one of the key drivers of them engaging because, as she puts it, 'If you are positive in your communication, including on the playground before and after school, they're much more likely to come and see you if there are any issues'. In other words, relationships at Littlecoates are built on praise, wherever it can be identified.

Teachers all take their classes out onto the playground at the end of the school day which provides them with a great chance to have a chat with parents, unless their pupils are in Years 5 or 6, in which case they are allowed to walk home alone. The termly parent-teacher meetings are also intended to encourage a dialogue, and they are held during the school day if it's convenient for parents but also after-school if they prefer, with as many appointments as possible being arranged close to the end of the school day. Children are welcome to come with their parents if there are childcare issues, and in the summer term sessions there is an opportunity for the parents to meet their child's new teacher. At the end of Neville's notes on this crucial component of the parent-school interface he reflects the teachers' determination to discuss their pupils' progress with parents with the following words: 'We pester any that don't sign up'. The word *pester* struck me as a positive verb in this context because I suspect that the parents are quietly pleased that their attendance is so sought after and their children's success so important to the school.

The idea of effective dialogue generating relationship is also exemplified by the home-school books that are used with some targeted children and families, consisting of two-way contributions from teaching assistants, teachers and parents to ensure clear communication, smooth daily transitions from home to school and back, as well as collaboration around learning intentions of course.

Relationships are often developed further when parents join in with extra-curricular activities. For example, a group of Littlecoates children traditionally takes part in the local singing festival, held annually at the Grimsby Auditorium, and parents always enjoy attending the performance at the end of these workshops. Emma also describes a recent, six-week DJ training project that has been provided for Year 6 pupils by the Grimsby Creates Noise initiative, culminating in an outdoor show in the town centre one Saturday afternoon, at which she remembers with real warmth a group of parents dancing along to their children's mixes.

Beaumont Hill

When the school came out of its COVID-19 bubbles recently Assistant Principal Helen started a face-to-face version of the parent forum that had been held online during the pandemic. She believes that parents of children with SEND tend to feel more isolated, and she was keen to help them to get together to socialise and network. She put on high tea which definitely

Figure 8.2 The principal of Littlecoates talking with a parent

helped to encourage attendance, and similar half-termly events are now becoming a regular feature on the calendar. Parental engagement has always been strong at Beaumont Hill, chiefly because daily communication with parents is always personalised to each child, due to their particular and highly individual health and educational needs. In those unusual cases where this hasn't been the case the wellbeing team has always been the first port of call for the leadership team. If parents aren't answering phone calls then staff from the welfare team are ready and willing to make a home visit and knock on doors to see if any help is needed to get the children to school.

Kirsty, early years and primary lead, explains that during the COVID pandemic, when parents didn't have other lines of support available, school was often their lifeline, a communication channel to vital services that couldn't easily be accessed directly by families, due to staff absences, the closure of GP surgeries and wider health precautions surrounding vulnerable children and adults. It was during this very difficult period that Kirsty believes many parents began to realise how much staff at Beaumont Hill are prepared to go above and beyond expectations, in their desire to support them. Examples included arranging contact with social workers, delivering a much-needed food parcel and picking up their child because the transport drivers were unwell. School staff readily took on tasks that aren't their prime responsibility, a willingness that Kirsty thinks made a massive impression on the parents receiving this support, and one which rapidly improved the parent-staff relationships that arose out of this highly challenging period for so many families, something that made the enormous staff workload highly rewarding at the time and legacy-building for the immediate future. One challenge facing Helen and the wider team is to find ways in which they can sustain these closer bonds between home and school and develop a similar partnership approach in those parents who are joining the school now, without the added catalyst of a pandemic.

Helen is keen to point out the role the school plays in helping parents to make connections and lifelines with each other, too, as such relationships are also vital to a sense of belonging. This social capital can allow parents of children on a similar learning pathway, such as PMLD (profound and multiple learning disability), not to feel alone when challenges arise, and can often provide the opportunity for signposting to additional support outside of school that can make all the difference to someone who feels 'at the end of their tether'. Feedback from parents has often stated the value of coffee mornings in providing parent-parent contact, the chief value of which is often seen as emotional and wellbeing support. Future plans for the parent forum include recruiting a named parent to be there for the parent body as a whole, able to field any individual's concerns and share them with Helen if appropriate.

Liaison with other local organisations is also a function of the forum, with one Beaumont Hill parent sitting on Darlington's 'Together for Better' parent carer forum. Some of the school's parents weren't aware of the range of support that's available to them until they began talking to this person, whose networking has helped to inform staff about what's out there as well. The 'Together for Better' initiative is also there to be used by the parents of those children who come to Beaumont Hill from other local authorities, recognising the valuable part that the school plays as a resource hub for its whole community, however widely spread.

Key ideas in this chapter

When reflecting on the six accounts above I have tried to pick out some of the actions and approaches that appear to have fostered a mutual sense of relationship between parents and schools most effectively. Some of them have been put forward by more than one of the schools chosen. As with other chapters there is space at the bottom of the list for you to add your own observations. You may also like to look back at the suggested model in Chapter 2 to see if any of them can be mapped onto the diagram that I have shared.

- Develop relationships with parents through meeting their needs in ways that they ask for and accept.
- Cement relationships through delivering popular and useful partnership events.
- Use a 'tough love' approach with parents where appropriate, but aim to move to a more equal and empowering relationship whenever possible.
- Help parents to develop a sense of belonging when they are in school.
- Use positive relationships to develop a 'word-of-mouth' or social media communication network amongst the parent community.
- Use links with appropriate local community groups to help build relationships with parents who attend them.
- Encourage staff to have conversations with parents through their accessibility at key times of the day, leading to more meaningful dialogue when needed.
- Evaluate the school site and website for the warmth of their welcome and make any necessary adjustments.

- Make use of those members of staff who have connected with particular families, allowing them to help colleagues to develop their own relationships with them.
- Remember the power of sharing food and drink in relationship building.
- Encourage and maintain practicable communication systems between staff and parents.
- Use joint learning activities to foster positive relationships between home and school and within families.
- Consider sharing appropriate information about staff to encourage parents to feel that they know and can approach them.
- Understand the link between relationship and expectation, paying attention to the nature of the expectations of school staff and of parents, and how each one perceives that they are being met by the other.
- Make use of good two-way communication to foster good relationships which in turn should lead to better parent involvement and engagement.
- Use extra-curricular activities as opportunities to develop relationships with parents.
- Recognise the lifeline that school can provide to isolated parents, using this to grow their interpersonal skills and help them to build supportive networks outside of school

You might like to add your own key ideas here from your reading in this chapter and any further thoughts about earlier material:

Conversation starters

Here are some follow-up questions to help you develop your own thinking about the ideas that I've proposed and any others that have been important to you in relation to securing effective parent partnership as widely as possible.

- In what ways do I as a practitioner, and we as a school, make effective relationships with parents as efficiently and speedily as possible?
- How do we encourage parents to get to know relevant school staff well enough to make relationships with them?
- How might we improve our relationship-building activity, based on the ideas and examples shared in this chapter and a wider reading of this book and other sources?

9 Trust

The reciprocal bond that arguably builds up through application of the previous four principles in the school's dealings with its parents, and which may need to be nurtured over time if is to be sustained

Rathfern

When Naheeda joined the Rathfern team as headteacher behaviour was frequently disrupting learning in the classroom, so she called a meeting for parents in the school hall which was very well attended. She remembers sharing in unflinching detail her plans for the school, describing how she intended to turn things round with the support of the staff team. She also remembers how negative many of the parents were about the school and how sceptical many of them were about her ideas. At the time many of the children who lived on the street that the school is built on didn't come to the school 'because they didn't think it was good enough'. It seems clear that, at the time, levels of trust in the school and its ability to keep children safe and educate them well were not high. However, Naheeda's experience in the subsequent 14 years of her leadership, shared by her evolving team, was that 'persistence pays off'.

The school's commitment to tackling systemic racism and to challenging default views about particular pupil groups has been unrelenting, a stance that has gradually gained the support of parents and built up their trust over time. In another example of the 'tough love' approach, lesson observations in the early days revealed what Naheeda considered to be too much therapeutic rather than academic work happening in classrooms, a balance that was quickly reset so that learning took centre stage and pastoral support delivered at other times and by other means.

The behaviour policy is under constant review at Rathfern to ensure that it's always following the best research evidence available, as well as ensuring that the trust that has been built up with parents is retained and deepened. Teachers and support staff throughout the school try really hard to disrupt ideas about who can be successful. For example, during nativity performances the 'usual contenders' will not always be taking the leading roles. Rather than focusing only on those children whose parents have been able to nurture their talents outside of school, staff are always keen to challenge what is referred to by some as the Matthew Effect, where those who have much tend to have even more added by societal systems such as schooling. At Rathfern, parts are often filled by those who will benefit most from them, an approach that builds parental trust in the school's determination to empower and develop all of its pupils without fear or favour.

Another effect cited by Naheeda is the Pygmalion or Rosenthal effect, by which a teacher's expectations of their pupils, whether positive or negative, can lead to a self-fulfilling prophecy. By this principle it is thought that giving children roles and tasks with high expectations of their ability to succeed can positively influence the outcomes, although some have called it into question, and common sense suggests that there will be limitations to this idea. In respect of the trust engendered in parent partnership, a balance may have to be struck between developing and nurturing existing talent as well as fostering latent potential where it can be identified.

As suggested above, Naheeda and her staff team are committed to challenging dominant narratives of communities of colour and disadvantage, an aspiration that is borne out during a virtual conversation with two current mums, and one former mum whose child has returned to the school for student practice, so fond are her memories of the place. The mums are all very complimentary about the school's approach to parent partnership during the time that they have had children there. It's clear that they feel that all children leave Rathfern with the same positive attitude to their learning and life chances, believing that can succeed, whatever their background.

One of the mums transferred her child with SEND to the school, having previously experienced considerable negativity almost every time she came to the school gate to collect him at the end of the day, as well as being disappointed at the way his EHCP was being administered. By contrast she has found the Rathfern staff to be positive, keen to ensure that her son's needs are met in ways that don't draw attention to his invisible disability, and prepared to listen to her and respond if she feels that he has any issues either at home or in school. As she puts it, 'He was allowed to be the same as everyone else'. She has recently become a parent governor at Rathfern and now enjoys accompanying children on educational visits as well as becoming more involved in working with Naheeda and the rest of the governing body as they decide the strategic direction of the school.

Two of the parents were unashamed to share the fact that the school receives Pupil Premium funding for their children, explaining that there is no stigma attached as far as they are aware. Real openness and honesty are evident in the exchanges that Naheeda has with the parents during our remote discussion, such as when one mum recalls a classroom incident involving her child that she feels was dealt with really well by the school, including Naheeda listening respectfully to the mum's views. She remembered saying at the time that the school's commendable inclusivity 'can be a problem if it impacts on other children's learning and wellbeing'. Naheeda recalls that the school 'learnt so much' from the interaction, an attitude that speaks volumes about her willingness to demonstrate openness and honesty in her dealings with parents and to model that approach to members of the staff team.

The mums all recognise language from school that is readily used by their children at home, such as the 'Red Zone' which one of the mums described herself as using with her children at times, when referring to her own need to 'walk away' for some cooling-off time. All of the parents, especially the mum whose children are now in their teens, recognise Rathfern's ability to develop in their children the ability to 'self-regulate and learn independently', assets that 'travel with them' as they transition successfully to their various secondary schools.

Naheeda regards this as 'school-proofing' the pupils so that they are ready to deal with any teachers in the secondary phase who might realistically be unfair or unkind to them.

When asked about their children's dad's or stepdad's willingness to come into school the mums quickly pointed out the popularity of the Forest School initiative in this respect, which allows opportunities for outdoor, active support for learning from men. Naheeda provided an encouraging example of one dad's involvement in her latest parent partnership project – 'Conversations about Race' – during which he made several confident and thought-provoking contributions to a general discussion with other parents. She was particularly pleased at his participation, coming as it did from a personal invitation from her to attend. Perhaps Naheeda's willingness to make a direct approach is one of the keys to tackling what many schools describe as a particular challenge in the whole area of parental involvement and engagement – getting dads into school. We will return to this theme in the final chapter.

In a recent Ofsted report on the school the following comment was made which seems to sum up very succinctly how trust is built up during a parent's association with Rathfern:

> Parents and carers appreciate how leaders communicate with them to offer help and support. They are proud of being part of the school. They like that the school clearly tells them about their child's learning. Parents said that their children are incredibly happy at school.
> (Ofsted 2021)

Chiltern

It's a mark of how well the school is thought of that a number of parents whose children have moved on to secondary school next door ask if they can still come to The Hub so that they can access the pantry. The trust built up over many years, alongside the knowledge of what the staff team can offer in ways that amount to much more than food, is clearly in their minds.

Sadly, there is a relatively high incidence of domestic abuse in the local area, so groups like the school's 'Bump to Baby' group can be an important resource to women who need access to people that they can trust. Staff are equally open to dads who face similar challenges, with opportunities to talk being provided on an informal basis.

Parents of children with additional needs form a particularly strong bond of trust with staff, and the head of school, Jacqui, fondly remembers one dad of a Year 6 pupil who cried when he saw a teacher running along beside her so that she could complete her cycling proficiency. She had come into nursery with plaster casts on both legs eight years earlier, and Dad declared through his tears, 'I never thought I'd see her ride a bike'.

The school is committed to taking as many children as possible to museums, the seaside and repeated swimming lessons in Years 5 and 6 if they haven't managed to learn in Year 4. All of this life-enhancing, and potentially life-saving, provision is welcomed by the parents, again based on the trust that is demonstrated amply in conversations that I have had with some of them. One dad told me that his daughter enjoys coming all the time, and he understands that she is doing 'quite well' as he put it. He feels that of the five positive parent partnership characteristics that I have proposed in this book, *relationship* is the most important one as far as he's concerned.

One of the mums that I spoke to describes the teachers as 'easy to get on with' and goes on to say that 'they'll listen to you, and do everything they can to resolve any issues'. She describes the parent-engagement staff as having plenty of ideas for helping children. Of the five characteristics included in this and preceding chapters she feels that *communication* is the key for her, especially from teachers to parents. She describes Eduspot, the school's communication system, as being excellent for payments and notices but also appreciates the text messages and phone calls staff make ample use of in the excellent support that they provide to parents. I speak to a couple who are highly appreciative of Chat and Choose, especially the opportunities that it has given them to meet and get to know other parents.

For another mum the word 'community' is at the centre of everything at Chiltern, something that she appreciates, as that's what she sees as the chief attraction of the local area, having lived there all her life, and indeed come to Chiltern herself as a child. She feels that the school encourages her daughter to have high aspirations for her future, and she would be happy whether her daughter travels the world or stays in Hull because, as she put it, 'it's what you are as a person that makes you'. In her view the school promotes this sentiment, too, which is a prime example of the shared approach that she feels the school takes since it deals with her daughter in the same way as she would at home. This synchronicity struck me as a real strength from this particular mum's point of view, and it makes me wonder how universal this view might be amongst parents more widely in England, and indeed beyond.

For the last couple whom I met during my visit to Chiltern the positive environment in the school, the centrality of wellbeing in its educational offer and the tendency of the staff to 'do whatever they can for whoever they can' are all factors that have led to great satisfaction. They are pleased that pressure from external sources isn't passed on to the children so that their son was allowed to make progress at his own pace, at a time when this was the most important consideration for them. They have also picked up the importance of growth mindset and are hugely impressed that whatever the school sets out to do for their children ultimately 'it does what it says'. This delivering on promises appears to have been crucial in building up trust relatively quickly for these two parents, whose children had joined the school relatively recently.

Initially, during the new leadership team's thrust to develop parent partnership, the staff were the ones saying all the 'hellos', whereas now the parents are much more prepared to initiate interactions with staff during the 15-minute 'soft start' (as executive headteacher Kath calls it) that begins each day. According to her the parents' faces are noticeably more relaxed, as they move through the school, than they were when she became involved at Chiltern. She goes on to say, 'Parents are expecting to be welcomed, not expecting to have difficulty. You can smile a bit if you're not on the defensive'. As she says this it would be easy to imagine that this is true only of the parents, but such is the nature of the mutual trust established over recent years that I can recognise how true this is of the staff too.

Ofsted inspectors were confident in 2019 to observe the following in the school's report to Kath:

> Your knowledgeable and committed assistant headteacher works hard with the community to ensure that aspirations and levels of engagement with school are high. The 'chat and choose' initiative and various workshops for parents are examples of effective engagement with parents, not only for improving standards of living in the community, but also for brokering support for families from external agencies and improving employment prospects.

98 Trust

Figure 9.1 Chiltern families share a meal and craft activities

As Jacqui puts it, 'We do everything for everybody as best we possibly can, often subtly', and it's this sensitivity that it seems to me is the crowning virtue of all the other Chiltern characteristics that I've described in previous chapters, and potentially the one most likely to lead to parental trust. The unobtrusive help offered to so many clearly means a great deal and contributes to genuine feelings of shared endeavour in their child's learning.

Sometimes families reach such a point that social-care professionals become heavily involved, as happened with one couple who were moved out of their house so that it could be completely cleared, refurbished and refurnished, ready for them to move back in with their children, with strict support initially in place from the local authority team. When social care withdrew their support on a phased basis it was Chiltern staff whom the parents trusted enough to allow them to step in and visit the home every fortnight in order to help them maintain the new habits and systems that allowed them to turn their lives around and provide the conditions that their children needed to thrive. My research conversation with the parent partnership team concludes with this statement from one of them, arising out of five years or so of relentless but hugely rewarding effort: 'Always be honest and truthful because parents can see through flannel!'

Brunel

As far as assistant head Paul is concerned, trust is the key to parental involvement and engagement which was something that emerged from the initial conversation that we had while I was preparing my original presentation on the subject. As I have suggested already, it isn't usually the first principle or characteristic that can be said to be present for a parent or a member of school staff because it usually takes time to develop. As Paul observes, trust from children and parents is built up through a myriad of small undertakings and demonstrations of positive, can-do attitude. As he says, 'If they ask you to do something, you're going to do it. You must do it, and then go back and tell them you've done it. Full circle. If you do that a couple of times, they then see you as someone they can trust to get things done'.

Of course, it's more complicated than this, but this seems like as good a place to start as any because proving to a parent that you have efficacy is also likely to convince them that ultimately they and their child matter to you. When I asked him which way round he feels the trust bond between a parent or a child and a teacher comes in terms of being the driving factor, he suggests that a parent is likely to be more receptive of a teacher's advances if their child is able to trust them or demonstrates that they like them. In his experience, especially in the years he's spent in different roles at Brunel, each trusting link made with a parent-child pairing is likely to lead to another one, and so on. By word of mouth, through friendships in the classroom and at the school gate, the idea soon spreads that if you have a conversation about something with this member of staff something will be done about it.

The level of trust that develops over a long period of time can then be harnessed when difficulties and challenges arise. In returning to the school in a leadership role Paul has been able to draw on a relatively long history of interactions with parents, with some of his current parents having been pupils of his when he started teaching. He is not alone in this, as a number of key staff have also been associated with Brunel for a relatively long time. Paul talks about one example of a child who had been excluded for a fixed term, where the mum felt secure enough to use a follow-up conversation with a member of staff to disclose a safeguarding issue for the first time, which in turn enabled the school to address the issue raised.

He remembers that, during the pandemic, if families didn't have something the school loaned it or gave it to them: IT equipment, paper, books, pens. A store was set up in an accessible part of the school site with the clear message, 'Come and help yourself', and parents did. Significantly, the trust shown in this way by the school to the parents involved has meant that the vast majority of what wasn't consumed has been returned. There is still a uniform rail as a legacy of those difficult times, which parents can access to reuse and recycle items in good condition.

Once trust has been secured Paul has some clear pointers as to how to retain it, especially in those situations where behaviour in school has been an issue. His advice arises out of wide experience of such encounters, and it can be summarised in the following paragraph:

Don't approach a parent with a stern face with the words 'You won't believe what he's done today!' Rather, start with a positive (assuming that there's one to be found) and then explain calmly and dispassionately what the child has done. Next, show empathy with the child by explaining that you understand why it happened (if there is an evident motivation for the action). After that, point out practically and ethically 'why we can't have that sort of behaviour in the school', and finally, let the parent know what the consequences or sanctions are for their child, in order to 'put it right'. Also, of course, provide opportunities for the parent to respond and make it clear that you've heard what they've said, even if you aren't able to agree with it. As Paul puts it, 'The conversation has been had', and both parent and child can hopefully move on constructively. It's also helpful he says to find the very next opportunity to give the parent some positive feedback about their child, again with a face-to-face conversation if possible, so that this interaction matches the context of the first one.

I can well remember, from my own years in school leadership, the look of pure relief on a parent's face when I was able to speak to them at the school gate, or on a home visit, about something that they could be proud of in their child's learning or behaviour, instead of the anticipated, all-too-frequent bad news. All of the above might be time-consuming and may have to be repeated, but approaches like this can often be responsible for a deepening of trust in the family's relationship with the school and may contribute to a child turning its behaviour round, supported as it is by a team approach from all the adults around it.

In a virtual conversation with Suzanne and three of the school's mums I discovered the value that is placed at Brunel on allowing children to learn about the whole of life, not just the academic aspects. It welcomes diversity, acceptance of others and is a welcoming environment. One of the mums is delighted that her child 'skips in and skips out', and another put great store by the fact that her child is happy and settled. At primary age especially, in her view, 'enjoying the learning' is paramount and something that Brunel excels at.

The mums feel that the school gets the balance just right between putting enough expectation on them to support the children's learning in school, whilst also keeping the 'friendly, family feel' that allows them to come readily into school to discuss and join in with their child's learning. One of the mums was particularly proud to support a group of children at a local sporting event, where other parents had commented on the high quality of the Brunel pupils' behaviour. Another aspect of the school's ethos was mentioned with great appreciation – the tendency to select children to attend sporting events, such as swimming galas, on the basis of what they would get out of participating, rather than the likelihood of them winning. For this group of mums the opportunities that are clearly available to all the children really endear them to it as the place where they have chosen for their children to be educated.

In reflecting on the home-schooling that had been forced on them by the pandemic the mums were universally complimentary, especially for the understanding mentality from teachers that one summarised as 'do what you feel you can manage', given that many of the parents were also trying to work from home at the time. The approachability of staff was also singled out as a strength, and the links made during the various lockdowns have increased this perception in lasting ways. As one put it, 'I don't worry about emailing somebody'. I was told about one pupil who, as the result of one such piece of home-school communication, suddenly announced that they wanted to make a model at home about what they had been studying.

Headteacher Suzanne speaks very fondly and proudly about the Facebook group that is run and managed by the parents. It's apparent that she believes the trust placed in the organisers and contributors goes on to bear fantastic fruit in the wider parent community, encouraging anyone and everyone to buy into all that Brunel has to offer. The ultimate evidence of this widespread faith in the school is encapsulated in this final statement from a 'satisfied customer': 'I just know that when my son goes in, I don't have to worry about anything'.

Carrington

In terms of building up trust Headteacher Kate suggests that, primarily, parents need to know that you'll deliver what you say you'll deliver, whether you are a school leader, teacher, teaching assistant, early years professional or administrator. When asked about whether relationship comes before trust, or *vice versa*, Kate suggests that it depends on the person, as she can think of examples of both from her career. In her interactions with her Class Parents group, she is aware of using them sometimes almost as a focus group. 'I'm thinking of doing this. What do you think?' This is an attitude that suggests a great deal of trust on her part, in that she is handing over some of the responsibility for decision-making to the parents attending, in much the same way as she would to the school's governing body. Having said their piece they in turn trust Kate to make what she ultimately sees as the best decision, based partly on their responses but also on those of other stakeholders.

Kate agrees with the premise that at best the principles or characteristics proposed in this book develop mutually. As much as she and her team strive to earn the trust of the parents at Carrington by their actions and attitudes, in trying to develop a genuine partnership with every one of them, she concludes our conversation with these telling words about her own leadership: 'It's about me trusting that the parents will do what they say they'll do'.

When I meet in a video call with Kate and a group of four parents, all mums, it's immediately obvious that they are all very comfortable with each other, and that openness and honesty are at the heart of the discussion. Kate makes it clear at the outset that she wants to hear about ways in which she and the rest of the staff can deliver even better parental involvement and engagement practices and systems, as well as to be encouraged about what they feel the school is getting right.

One mum talks immediately about the many opportunities that she is given at Carrington to speak to teachers about her child, enjoying genuine dialogue about issues that matter in relation to their learning and broader aspects of family life if needed. She feels that she can speak readily to Kate, often by ringing her, and describes her as 'really warm', knowing all the children by name, and even some of the siblings who don't come to the school. As a full-time working mother of two she has been able to volunteer to support educational visits occasionally, such as on a recent trip to Beale Wildlife Park in Reading, but feels that the balance is just right between the school's offer to parents to become involved as much as they feel able, alongside not expecting more from them than they can give.

Another mum, who describes herself as neurodivergent, talks about the contrast between her child's previous school, where there had been a complete relationship breakdown with the headteacher, and her experiences with Kate at Carrington. She finds now that she can cautiously but confidently express her views to Kate and other school staff and have them listened to, respected and validated. She feels much clearer about where she stands in these relationships and no longer feels terrified that she's going to be made to feel foolish, especially in front of her children. She summarises her first encounters with Kate like this: 'I wasn't made to feel like I was a problem'. Since becoming a parent at the school this mum has been affirmed for her deep knowledge and understanding of autism because of Kate's willingness to ask her for help with issues that arise in her own professional encounters with the condition, and it's clear that this recognition of expertise not only develops Kate's ability to empathise with other parents and children, but also deepens the trust between the two of them.

A third mum picks out as resonating with her, my suggestion, early in the discussion, that parents are a child's first teacher. Her experiences during the COVID-19 lockdowns brought this idea back very strongly for her, as she was supporting her child's learning and trying to find ways to do that when, inevitably, staff weren't on hand virtually for advice on which methods and techniques to try. Looking back she realises how quickly communications to and from Carrington became creative and multi-faceted, with the use of video clips and live online lessons rapidly being adopted by staff and parents as they strove, with increasing success, to deliver effective learning experiences for those children who were not able to be in school. The two-way trust that was fostered during the many new challenges and experiences thrown at homes and the school during the pandemic will hopefully be sustained as families move through the system, during and beyond their relatively brief time at Carrington, and the school may be able to continue some of the skills learned and methods mastered, whilst recognising that there is no real substitute for face-to-face classroom learning experiences.

According to the parents there are layers of communication and layers of engagement at the school, with plenty of one-to-one communication with Kate and other members of the leadership team when the need arises or when there is particularly good news to impart. When problems arise they tell me that their views are invariably 'embraced, welcomed and worked through'. Another feature of Kate's headship is that she's 'always asking for feedback', from anyone who will listen it seems. The mums involved in the discussion recognise that there is a group of parents who find it harder to establish the relationship that they enjoy with the school, possibly because they feel that the staff and governors aren't 'walking in their shoes' or maybe due to their own feelings of fear or lack of worth. As a group, they support the notion that Kate and her staff team's determination to be available, understand, validate and engage every single parent is all that can be done to steadily overcome this barrier.

One of the mums has recognised that she has become something of a conduit for the views of other parents, or a 'Year One figurehead' as Kate puts it. She feels that in matters affecting her child's learning she has 'an equal voice'. She goes on to describe what she sees as a triangle of responsibility shared by the children, the teaching and learning staff and the parents. She remembers a recent example when, due to COVID restrictions, there was no Year One Christmas performance planned, but Kate was humble enough to listen to representations from parents and to agree to putting something on safely to ensure that the children and families didn't miss out. The parents appear to respect the fact that senior staff are prepared to listen, reflect and sometimes (but not always) change their minds.

During the discussion Kate's views as Carrington's headteacher begin to emerge with real clarity. Her inclination is to share any news of intended changes with parents before staff, a tendency that she's aware can be controversial with her colleagues sometimes. Her reasoning is that parents are the most invested stakeholders in a child's education. As she says to the mums who are participating in our virtual discussion, 'You are the voices for your children', which is perhaps especially true in an infant school like Carrington, where the children are younger and generally less confident than those higher up in the primary phase.

The final voice comes from a mum who had also had a difficult time at her child's previous school but who discovered a completely different ethos at Carrington. She fondly remembers sitting next to Kate as they waited to go into on one of the mum's first school events and hearing this very different headteacher quietly say to her, 'My door's always open if you want a cup of tea'. She wasn't in a great place personally at the time, and she almost felt like crying. At that moment she most needed to feel heard and to know that someone had the time to say, 'How are you?' This mum has gone on to be a regular participant in Kate's 'Class Parent' sessions, where all the mums say that their voices are heard and their ideas taken seriously. Kate's experience so far, with groups like this, is that some year group's parents gel as a galvanised whole, whereas it's harder with others to encourage this feeling of togetherness, or to identify any individuals who have the trust of the group, and who might go on to become voices for those who are reluctant to come forward themselves. The group of mums that I meet definitely see the value of the forum that Kate provides in her Class Parent group and are clearly keen to encourage others to come and find the mutually trusting environment that they relish being part of, even for the relatively short duration of a child's infant school career.

Figure 9.2 A Carrington parent reads with her child

Littlecoates

Staff throughout the school are well-aware of the huge responsibility they all have to keep the children in their care safe, as well as to teach them and support their learning, so it's not a surprise to discover that they always call parents to let them know if their child has had an injury or been involved in a serious behaviour incident. This kind of openness inevitably leads to increased levels of trust, as parents are secure in the knowledge that they will be kept informed of anything that might affect their child's happiness or wellbeing. The school is beginning to look at restorative approaches to resolve behaviour issues between children so that they can move from discussing good or bad choices, along with the idea that actions lead to predetermined consequences, to thinking about who has been affected and deciding what they (the perpetrator and the recipient) can do to make it better.

During a brief visit to the school I meet with the principal, Neville, and a group of three mums, who share with me their views about parent partnership at Littlecoates. Neville offers to leave, but the parents are adamant that they are happy to speak openly and honestly in front of him, and I sense his readiness to listen in on our conversation, to contribute if asked and to take away any positive feedback to share with his team. He is also keen, he tells us, to learn from anything they say that might inform future strategy in this key area, and even though during the time that I'm there nothing worthy of note comes up, I get the impression that these are people whose suggestions for improvements have been listened to seriously before, and will be again in the future.

One of the mums begins by sharing a few brief episodes in her child's learning journey at Littlecoates, including their transfer to the school, immediate investigation into a possible special educational need and the timely provision of extra support before additional funding could be secured. Throughout this settling-in period Mum felt like a genuine part of the team around her child in ways that she didn't in their previous school. As another mum puts it, 'I feel like they [the staff] believe they wouldn't manage without us'. Her child moved to the school with a speech impediment which the teacher, a speech and language therapist and Mum, along with members of the support staff, worked together to overcome. Within six months the child had been discharged from therapeutic interventions and has since taken part in class assemblies and other performances with increasing confidence and ability. The response of staff to any child with additional needs appears to be the following attitude, stated by one of the mums in a way that implies that the school is not looking for excuses: 'So what?' If needs be, staff will push children to achieve at their own level no matter what, and they are able to understand people from all walks of life. The parents appear to trust the school team because of the encouraging and supportive way in which this 'push' is delivered.

In describing the staff at all levels the parents say that 'They don't come across as superior to you, they won't be beaten, and they pool their resources to help your child achieve'. They have observed that members of staff are aware of each other's knowledge and skills, and aren't afraid to ask for help from colleagues if it's needed. Communication before the COVID-19 pandemic is described as good, but the parents are convinced that it has improved as a result of the lockdowns being imposed. They seem particularly pleased with the school's adoption of the ClassDojo system, informing me that it's really easy to get in touch with staff these days, as well as to post pictures of their children's exploits at home if they wish. All of them speak highly of the school business manager, Dawn, describing her as 'the hub of the school' and perhaps by implication the person in whom the greatest trust is invested by the group, given her length of service and the number of times that she has 'been there for them' behind the welcoming counter in reception.

A phrase that comes up several times is 'they care', for example when the school quietly replaces a pair of shoes for a child whose parents are struggling to do so themselves or by the simple act of a member of staff ringing a parent to ask how their older child's operation has gone in Sheffield. This tendency to act in ways that 'they didn't have to' strikes me as one of the characteristics of the school that most endears the mums to it. 'The culture starts at the top', they claim, leading to a thoroughly inclusive feel around the school, where it's clear from details like the presence of a Romanian-speaking teaching assistant, or the SENDCo's apparent ability to pull in resources from everywhere, that diversity is genuinely welcomed. Another factor that comes across is the incredible resilience of staff during what has been a very challenging period, although it seems that this characteristic has been amply demonstrated to all three mums throughout their children's time at the school.

It seems appropriate to leave the last word about parent partnership at Littlecoates to the Ofsted inspector whose visit clearly picked up the underlying trust that I find during my own encounters with the school community.

> Parents and carers share pupils' extremely positive view of the school. A typical comment on Parent View, Ofsted's online questionnaire for parents, praised the commitment of all staff, describing Littlecoates Primary as a 'fabulous school where the staff go above and beyond'. Parents of children in the early years value how well their children settle into school because of the care and attention given by staff.
>
> (Ofsted 2019)

Beaumont Hill

In one of our emails discussing parent partnership in the school Assistant Principal Helen points out the importance of using the term 'parents/carers' in all communications with those adults with whom the children live. This practice is common in all of the schools included in these case-study chapters, but she pointed it out as being especially important in the case of a special school like Beaumont Hill, where there appears to be a higher proportion of alternative family arrangements than is generally the case in the mainstream primary sector. It is by paying attention to small details like this, and by taking the trouble and care of showing that she knows during individual conversations what the relationship is between adult and child, that trust is secured and maintained.

It is clear from joining the predominantly face-to-face parent forum, via a Teams link on the big screen in the school hall, that there is a great deal of trust between the parents and staff present. Helen explains that most of the parents who attend the meetings have children in the early years and primary classes because by the time that children have moved up into the secondary phase they are more used to the school's systems, and know members of the staff team well enough to be able to approach them about any issues in their child's lives. As one member of staff puts it, 'They trust the school just to get on with it, based on their previous experiences'. The school provides for children from two to 19 years, during which time a lot of capital is being built up, and as children move through the school parents tend only to get in touch if they perceive that something is going wrong. The trusting relationship that has generally been built up by the end of year six contrasts strongly with that which starts from scratch when pupils join Beaumont Hill at the beginning of Key Stage Three, which is often the case. If parents join the school with their child at other points during their time in early years or primary Kirsty, the assistant principal who leads these phases, will frequently accompany them to one of the weekly drop-ins that are advertised on the school's private parent Facebook page, with the catchy message, 'Come along and join us for an informal chat and refreshments'. She and Helen have found this to be a really effective way of encouraging a variety of parents to attend these sessions when, as Kirsty puts it, 'They need their voice to be heard'. The message that comes across strongly from both colleagues about the drop-ins, and the less frequent but more focused parent forum afternoons, is that it's 'all down to trust'.

Helen manages to gather some considered written parent quotes from some of those present during the forum that I am invited to join via Teams, and they include the following, based on the parents' views about the key principles that I'd shown them on the big screen: 'Parents should *respect* the wealth of knowledge, experience, sacrifice and good intentions of the school staff. School should be able to respect the sometimes differing opinions and decisions of the family when making joint plans for the child' (emphasis added).

Another interesting observation, this time about *knowledge*, is:

It is essential for parents and teachers to share knowledge. Both will have information from the professionals involved in the child's care along with research they have gathered. The teachers will have a wealth of knowledge they have gained in their training and professional experience, which will go hand in hand with the parent's knowledge that is unique to their personal experience with their child and what they have displayed and experienced since birth and when outside of school.

A key attribute for school staff, and parents if it is another reciprocal trait, comes one step before being able to understand and empathise which is *listening*. As a parent movingly puts it:

> As a parent there's no one else who gets what you are going through as a family other than the staff at school or other parents in the same situation as yourself. As a parent of two children with complex needs it's important to have someone to offload to and not be judged and also for it to be kept confidential. The staff at school just get it and understand how hard it can be for families. More often than not the staff have already come across the barriers our families face on a daily basis and do give us solutions to try which is always a relief and also other parents can offer their advice too. Having children with complex needs can be very isolating so attending the parent carer drop-ins at school and talking to staff and other parents is a lifeline for us families.

With regard to *understanding and empathy* one parent also sees this as a two-way street, writing: 'Staff must have high levels of empathy to even enter into this field. They must also practise self-care and self-awareness about compassion fatigue or burnout'. They went on to suggest that 'parents need to be compassionate towards teachers who care for multiple, often physically and emotionally demanding and complex children. Not to mention the compounded grief over time of multiple bereavements and safeguarding incidents. Parents should understand that this is not just a *job* for these teachers, this is often their life's passion and so something they are emotionally invested in'.

In respect of the importance of *relationship* one parent writes this:

> It's important to have a close relationship with school staff so you can both work together and work out what's right and wrong for the child's needs because at the end of the day you both want a happy and positive outcome for the child. It's also good to have a good relationship with school because sometimes school is the only support a parent has.

Finally, we come to *trust*, potentially a product of all that has come before, as I have suggested in Chapter 3. Two of the Beaumont Hill parents come up with the following statements on this characteristic:

> It's hard to overstate the importance of trust when a parent is choosing any caring environment for their child. This is even more profound when the child has additional needs. The base level of trust initially required is much higher and can be tested over time if the child's behaviour, or mental or physical health dips while in the school's care. There is also an unspoken expectation that staff can trust parents to inform them of anything that could affect other students or alter the level of care the child require.

> It's important to trust the staff members at school because you are leaving the most precious thing a parent has in the hands of another to look after them and care for their needs.

When I speak later via Zoom to Beaumont Hill's executive principal, Caroline, she tells me that it's her responsibility, with the school's staff team, of course, to overcome any challenges that get in the way of 'making education work' for each and every pupil. This includes making sure that communication from school to home, and *vice versa*, is bespoke to the family, she explains. She points out that what is required for each set of parents or carers can change quite a lot over time, especially in the primary phase when the child and family are still establishing patterns of behaviour with the school, and when health changes can be quite sudden. At such points Caroline sees it as the school's responsibility to take the lead in modifying how they pass on and receive information, rather than leaving it solely to the parents to find a way through any difficulties.

She sees building parent partnership as remarkably straightforward and distils it down to something like this: 'Build relationships and communicate effectively'.

Another key aspect that Caroline picks out of the suggestions included in Figure 3.1 is the need to be transparent, especially if something goes wrong at school. Her formula with parents on such occasions is to accept that it shouldn't have happened, explain what is going to be done about it, see that through and then finally, share any outcomes where appropriate.

She often says to parents who may have concerns about their child's education at Beaumont Hill, 'We will always do our best, but we won't always get it right'. She is also keen to point out that if parents would like to tell the school how they think they might do a better job, school staff will listen. After all, she tells me, 'Parents are their child's first teacher and usually their strongest advocate'.

The school's Ofsted journey over recent years, taking it rapidly from an 'inadequate' judgement to a categorisation of 'good', can be summarised by two extracts from inspection reports that were written just 22 months apart:

> The parents who spoke to inspectors were unequivocally positive about the school's effectiveness. Parents spoke about the effectiveness of communication between home and school and the helpful advice and support they receive from teachers and senior leaders. Some parents highlighted the value of information and training they have received about how to stay safe when using computers and the internet. The views of parents who responded to Parent View, Ofsted's online questionnaire, and those who made written comments were more mixed. Some parents did not agree that their children are taught well or that they are making good progress. Similarly, some parents indicated that the school does not respond well to the concerns they raise.
>
> (Ofsted 2017)

And then:

> Parents and carers spoken to and those who completed Ofsted's online questionnaire Parent View held positive views on the quality of care and provision for their children.
>
> (Ofsted 2018)

It's clear from my conversations with Caroline, Helen and Kirsty, as with all of the staff in the schools that I visited either physically or virtually, that one of the key principles is not to sit back on a positive external judgement like this one, but instead to strive constantly to do better with parental involvement and engagement. It is perhaps this attitude above anything else that is most likely to foster the *trust* that I have tried to focus on in the case study contributions contained in this chapter.

Key ideas in this chapter

When reflecting on the six accounts above I have tried to pick out some of the actions and approaches that appear to have fostered mutual trust in the parent-school relationship most effectively. Some of them have been put forward by more than one of the schools chosen. As with other chapters there is space at the bottom of the list for you to add your own observations. You may also like to look back at the suggested model in Chapter 2 to see if any of them can be mapped onto the diagram that I have shared.

- Periodically review key policies, such as that covering behaviour, to ensure that the trust that has been built up is retained.
- Ensure that parents can clearly see how equality of opportunity applies to their child in school.
- Challenge dominant narratives with parents when they are in danger of holding their child's learning back.
- Act with openness and honesty in all dealings with parents.
- Try to make the time to listen carefully to parents, and act on what has been heard whenever possible.

- Deliver on promises to parents, and share with them how you have done that.
- Build up trust with parent-child pairings so that they can feed off each other's view of the school or member of staff.
- Show trust in parents' ability to deliver agreed support or return shared resources.
- Temper negative feedback to parents with opportunities for praise so that they are less likely to perceive you as prejudiced against them and their child.
- Have realistic expectations of the support with learning that individual parents can give to their child.
- Delegate appropriate tasks to capable parents, such as Facebook page administration, with the confidence that demonstrates belief in their abilities.
- Ask parents how they would improve the school's educational and extra-curricular offer to children and families and demonstrate how their ideas have been given genuine consideration, especially when they have not been adopted.
- When problems arise with a child's learning or behaviour, embrace, welcome and work through their parents' views.
- Demonstrate clearly to parents the school's commitment to keeping children as safe as possible.
- Push each child's learning in a way that individual parents see as supportive and encouraging.
- Show parents that you care for and about their children.
- Get details right in communications to show that you really know the child and their family.
- Be transparent when things go wrong for a child in school, and always demonstrate how staff have sought to do their best, even when they haven't managed to get it right.

You might like to add your own key ideas here from your reading in this chapter and any further thoughts about earlier material:

Conversation starters

Here are some follow-up questions to help you develop your own thinking about the ideas that I've proposed and any others that have been important to you in relation to securing effective parent partnership as widely as possible.

- In what ways do I as a practitioner, and we as a school, build mutual trust with parents as efficiently and speedily as possible?
- In what ways have we seen trust eroded or completely broken recently and, on reflection, how might this have been avoided?
- How might we improve our trust-building activity, based on the ideas and examples shared in this chapter and a wider reading of this book and other sources?

Chapter 9 reference list

Ofsted (2017) *School Report: Beaumont Hill Academy*. Manchester: Ofsted
Ofsted (2018) *School Report: Beaumont Hill Academy*. Manchester: Ofsted
Ofsted (2019) *Short Inspection of Littlecoates Primary Academy*. Manchester: Ofsted.
Ofsted (2021) *Inspection of an outstanding school: Rathfern Primary School*. Manchester: Ofsted.

10 Conclusions and next steps for schools

What are we to make of all this? What does it mean for my educational practice? Where might we go next as a school?

Back in 2011 I remember visiting the school of a fellow headteacher in Grimsby after his school had been rated as inadequate and hearing his description of what it was like to work with an HMI (Her Majesty's Inspector) on his post-inspection action plan. We talked about data and its importance in the monitoring process, and he told me how the HMI constantly used the question, 'So what?' Later, as a consultant, I have encouraged my colleagues in school leadership and management to write a commentary on any data that they have gathered, followed by a fairly concise piece of text with the title 'Strategic Implications'.

Assuming that you've made it to the end of this book, hopefully having found at least some of the contents thought-provoking, informative and maybe even inspirational, my question to you is 'So what?' In other, less punchy words, 'What are the strategic implications of what you have read, thought and perhaps discussed with others?' How will you change your own practice or, if you are the leader of a primary school or academy, what will you aim to do differently throughout the school as a result?

One of the conclusions that I have reached in writing this book is that language has been used by different researchers and writers to mean slightly different things, so maybe I should give my reasons for choosing the book title that I have. Whether the terms 'parental involvement' and 'parent engagement' describe the same characteristic in a school's approach, and whether one comes before the other or not, are moot points I feel. For this reason I've chosen what I see as an all-embracing term that not only has the advantage of being alliterative, and therefore slightly more memorable, but also captures, as far as I'm concerned, what a school is seeking to achieve with its strategies in respect of its parents and carers. Ultimately, it seems to me, children will learn best if the adults in their school and those at home are working together to support their efforts. You may have noticed that I have included again the term *carers* in this paragraph, mostly because I do recognise that children are living in a variety of familial and institutional contexts, and in our communications with each and every one of them it's important that the adults who are responsible for their care feel included. At the point that we are drawing conclusions it seems important to reiterate this message, and I will return to this in a little more detail later.

In this the final chapter I'm going to address the questions that are stated after the title, starting with 'What are we to make of all this?' You may have made notes in the book as you've gone along or perhaps, as I would have done, you've followed your childhood instruction not to write in books and scribbled your ideas on paper or in some kind of learning log instead. Either way, you will have some thoughts and ideas about your own practice in school, or about the work of the staff as a whole if you are a school leader. As a trainer and consultant during the last ten years I have frequently suggested to colleagues that changing the behaviours of a staff and volunteer team is not easy, but I would like to propose the following responses, undertaken in the order suggested:

1 Carry out an audit. (Several are available commercially, and one, created by me, which I will refer to from now on, is included in the appendix.)
2 Devise some strategic responses that attempt to answer the question 'So what?' (These can be included in brief on your audit form and fleshed out in other documents such as your Pupil Premium Strategy or School Improvement Plan.)
3 Implement your responses (in limited pilot form wherever possible).
4 Monitor and evaluate the actions and approaches that you have implemented.
5 Roll out your successful strategies more widely if you began with a limited response (with any necessary modifications suggested).
6 Maintain and improve your parent partnership provision through constant low-key monitoring, evaluation and refinement.

This gradual, step-by-step approach to school improvement was suggested to me about eight years ago when I read John Kotter's book on the subject of organisational change, *Our Iceberg is Melting* (Kotter and Rathberger 2006), which was widely recommended at the time. Having researched Kotter's ideas more deeply I created a straightforward planning tool to support primary schools in using his approach to effect change in a particular area, such as metacognition and self-regulation or the use of teaching assistants. This planner proved popular with delegates on my courses and colleagues whom I worked with during my consultancy visits to schools, so I have included it in the appendix of this book, in case you or your leader would like to use it as you seek to effect change in your own school's parent partnership provision. It's self-explanatory I hope, but there is plenty of information about Kotter's approach on the internet if you'd like to find more background information, or further commentary about the purpose of each of the steps proposed.

Some of you may be in schools where parent partnership hasn't been identified as an issue, and you may well feel that 'if it ain't broke, don't fix it'. I would gently suggest that even though your parents and carers appear to be working with you as successfully as they might, by virtue of there being very few parental complaints, well-attended parents' evenings and a thriving PTA or friends group, it could well be possible that a little fine-tuning will lead to even better educational and emotional outcomes for your pupils, such is the estimated impact of successful parent partnership. We are now well into considering the second and third questions under the chapter heading, whether you are thinking about your own personal practice or that of your whole school. In the former case there are plenty of ideas in earlier chapters that you could try, with the permission of your school's leaders, of course, in which case you might become a unilateral pilot programme for the wider school. Parent partnership might even be an opportunity for you to show your willingness to participate in the kind of groundbreaking activity that will demonstrate your readiness for wider leadership.

The audit document arises from another popular management tool of mine, this time originally focussing on Pupil Premium, the English funding stream currently in place to try to close achievement gaps based on 'disadvantage' (the term used by Ofsted and the DfE to describe economic deprivation, and referred to earlier in this book). I have recently adapted this format to address parent partnership (ParPar is an admittedly corny abbreviation that a colleague and I came up with recently when completing the audit together, which also avoids replicating the 'PP' that most English schools use to represent Pupil Premium), and I will describe how you might use it to carry out a review of your current practice, as well as considering what improvements you will make in the future.

The audit is divided into three deliberately non-Ofsted columns, all of which in my opinion are worthy but hopefully incremental places for your school to be: developing, establishing and refining. For each of these column headings there are then four row titles, based on the following aspects of parent partnership: awareness, financial management, strategies and reporting.

1. Taking one of the four sections at a time RAG-rate the descriptors in each column using pink (this colour leaves the underlying words more legible than red does), orange and green marker pens. Green is for those descriptors that you feel are definitely accurate for your school's provision, orange for those that you feel you are on the way to achieving, and no highlighter for those phrases or sentences that you don't yet have in place. Your parents' circumstances may mean that the provision outlined would not be appropriate, in which case no highlight would clearly be appropriate. I would reserve pink highlights for those descriptors that you don't feel you have in place yet, especially those that I have included in the first column, but feel that you really should. This represents therefore a fairly urgent priority for you, where orange and un-highlighted suggest a longer timescale for improvement.

2. As you complete each row write briefly in the 'notes and evidence' sections a description of the documents, data and other sources (e.g. school website) that justify your decision about how you have highlighted the descriptors. As alluded to above this would also be the place to explain why some of the descriptors are not appropriate for your school, if that has been your view when completing the audit. In completing these sections electronically with colleagues I have always suggested using a plain black font so that the results of the third step will be distinct from this part of the audit process.

3. Having decided where the school's parent practice currently sits, it's now time to change the pen or font colour (blue or purple work quite well, being non-RAG colours) and record a small number of improvements that you'd like to make in the short to medium term (possibly twelve to 18 months), along with the person or people who will be responsible for overseeing or implementing the changes. The descriptors in each column are intended at this point to give you some possible ideas for actions and approaches to adopt or develop further. The basis for most of them can be found in the EEF guidance referenced in Chapter 1, with other additions from my wider research or from the school accounts that comprise Chapters 5 to 9. You might like to address any gaps in the first two columns initially, but if these are complete then there should be suggestions in the third column for you to aspire to.

Whilst creating the audit I was aware of how different it was to my previous Pupil Premium tool, in that so much of what is included relies heavily on actions outside of the school's control. This is because *partnership* with parents and carers is clearly at the heart of many of the judgements being made. This dilemma might be something else that you could address in the 'evidence and notes sections', including a commentary as to why some of your school's evidence is as it is. I suppose ultimately this is one of the biggest challenges inherent in striving for excellent parent partnership, but the aspiration is nevertheless a laudable one in my view.

As part of the audit process you might like to try using the four prompt questions that informed my own case-study research, or even go through the whole interview exercise, both of which can be found in Chapter 4, with a brief commentary on how you might use them and the amount of time that the process is likely to take. As I pointed out earlier, choosing an outsider from your trust or local authority to carry out some research in your own school, as I did with my six collaborating schools, would be a sensible way to keep costs down if a leader from your school is able to provide the reciprocal service. This would also have the advantage of giving them the opportunity to learn lessons from the other school and to reflect on your own practice while doing so.

Loose ends

I am aware of a number of loose ends that I have indicated I will address briefly in this final chapter. I recognise that all of them are worthy of being studied in greater depth, but this is beyond the scope of this book and is something that I will leave you to research for yourselves online, if they are of interest to you or pertinent to your school's context.

Engaging with dads

When I was working with the FAST (Families and Schools Together) programme a frequent topic of debate was the difficulty that many schools faced in encouraging dads to participate in partnership events. This is something that I had experienced in my own career in schools, and there are no ready answers. Talking recently (in my governor role) to some mums at a singing festival in Grimsby, it was suggested by them that dads are more inclined to see themselves as the family's primary earner and, therefore, to see school-associated tasks as less their responsibility and, therefore, less worthy of asking their employer for time off. They pointed out certain events in school, such as sports day and the fiercely contested dad's race, or working-party events to do with the fabric of the school and its site, such as building a sensory garden, as being more attractive in general to their partners. A cursory look at the internet reveals compelling research to suggest that when dads are involved in their children's education children achieve more highly, so this is an area for schools to continue to address, bearing in mind, of course, that the proxies for parent partnership (e.g. attendance at school events) are not necessarily the aspects of supporting learning that make the greatest difference. As we saw in Chapter 1 conversations between children and parents in the home, about learning, are what we are trying to encourage most. Of course, when looking to engage dads and other male carers or guardians more effectively, schools will have in mind the same-sex couples and the single and separated parents who make up their client or customer base.

Mental health and wellbeing

As a school counsellor for the last two years I have experienced first-hand the importance of good mental health to a child's success as a learner, and it's essential that parents are on-board with any support offered, especially with primary-aged children. All of the schools I worked with in writing this book recognised the need to consider signposting parents to support for their own mental health and wellbeing, recognising as they did that this aspect of family life can be another barrier to a child's learning when it's not addressed. A recent conversation with a member of the school nursing team in a city on the northeast of England revealed her enthusiasm about the *Solihull Approach* which has been adopted by the local authority concerned. It provides online training for parents, with separate courses for mums and dads on how to understand and support their child. This is an example of a partner service taking a lead in key aspects of parenting, wider than just the issue of mental health, which allows school staff to signpost, encourage parent participation and collaborate with what is on offer, where they have the capacity to do so.

Looked-after children

In England additional Pupil Premium funding is provided by the government for children who are currently in local authority care, or have been in the past, prior to their adoption. Each local authority has a virtual school head whose team oversees the spending of the funding on those pupils who are currently in care, using a PEP (Personal Education Plan) drawn up by the school. For adopted children the funding continues to be available, but schools have more freedom in how they spend it. Having worked with one local authority's looked-after children team as a pupil tutor I have seen first-hand the importance of schools engaging fully with foster parents and key workers in children's homes. Adoptive parents naturally appreciate being viewed as partners in their child's education just as much as their birth-parent counterparts, so it is essential that the school's knowledge of each child's circumstances allows them to approach the parent-school interface conscientiously for all parents and carers, grandparents, older siblings and other relatives, with the additional sensitivity that might be needed if a child's context is a challenging one.

Parent governors

I have mentioned parent governors a few times in the book, and I have had personal experience of very supportive and objective people in that role, who have been able to put their own child's interests to one side where necessary when contributing to strategic discussions. I have also encountered parent governors who have found that challenge too much for them, or who appear to have put themselves forward for the purpose of acquiring and exercising power, rather than participating in strategic conversations from the perspective of being a representative of the whole parent and carer group. One of the parents who participated in the case-study conversations is the chair of governors in her school and admitted to finding it hard at first to put her own child's interests to one side when difficult decisions had to be made. She now describes herself as being hooked by the role and declares herself to have found a real passion for education that wasn't there before. As a former headteacher my own memories of parent governors that I have worked alongside include many of them being concurrently my sternest critics and my strongest supporters. This helpful approach can be summed up in the phrase 'critical friend', a term often used in the past to describe the ideal governor. In respect of parent partnership, parent governors take on the crucial tasks of being advocates with their peers, contributing enormously to clear communication, and offering to support those parents and carers who are hesitant about coming forward with concerns. As far as I am concerned long may that continue.

Conversation starters

Here are some follow-up questions to help you to use the tools outlined in this chapter effectively, or to guide you through your own follow-up research.

- What audit tools are available to us, and which one shall we use?
- Who could we ask to support us in carrying out our audit honestly by providing independent insights?
- Is it possible to set up a reciprocal arrangement that will keep costs down and provide an opportunity for members of our staff to investigate the practice of another school?
- How good are we at engaging our dads in parent partnership activities, and how might we do this better?
- What steps do we take to support our parents' mental health and wellbeing? How could we improve this area of our own provision or our signposting of other services?
- Do we treat all our parents and carers fairly and equally, regardless of their relationship to the children they support?
- How well do we recruit and use our parent governors, and how might we develop this aspect of governance?

Chapter 10 reference list

Kotter, J. and Rathberger, H. (2006) *Our Iceberg Is Melting*. London: Macmillan

Appendix

PARENT PARTNERSHIP AUDIT FORM

School or academy: Date:

Area of provision	Developing	Establishing	Refining
Awareness of parent partnership and associated issues	School leaders are aware of parent* partnership as an important aspect of school life and one member of the leadership team has been identified as having responsibility for it. Recent reports on the subject from, for example, Ofsted, the DfE and the EEF have been downloaded and read but have not yet been acted upon fully. A policy is being written with governors. Some parents are aware of, and can use, the school's systems for encouraging partnership with them in support of their child's learning and wellbeing.	School leaders are aware of the likely impact of effective parent partnership on pupil outcomes and have successfully responded to recommendations in recent reports on the subject. An appropriate person has attended recent relevant training on the subject and is beginning to provide leadership based on what has been learnt. Leaders, teachers and other key staff understand the importance of working effectively with parents to secure the best pupil outcomes. Well-respected research evidence on parental involvement and engagement has been collected, read and is beginning to be acted on in small-scale trials or pilot schemes in order to evaluate the efficacy of any actions and approaches adopted. An effective policy has been approved by the governing body and is becoming embedded in practice. Most parents know how to use the school's systems successfully to involve themselves in their child's learning and foster in them a sense of wellbeing.	School leaders, including governors, and all relevant members of staff, are fully aware of parental involvement and engagement and precisely how they have been, and are currently being, delivered in the school. Recent reports on the subject have been read, understood and acted upon fully. A designated member of the leadership team has a precise understanding of how parent partnership contributes to strong pupil outcomes, and members of the governing body are able to explain to stakeholders how. Teachers and other key staff have embedded in their practice those principles, skills, personal attributes and attitudes that are conducive to effective parent partnership. Well-respected research evidence on parental involvement and engagement informs securely embedded actions and approaches, with constant review and adjustment if required. The school's policy has been reviewed at least once and closely reflects the practice of the vast majority of staff, governors and other volunteers. Almost all parents know about, and use, the school's systems highly effectively to support their child's learning and sense of wellbeing. Those who do not are sensitively targeted to participate more.

Notes and evidence with next steps planned:

Financial management of parent partnership activities and approaches	Spending related to parent partnership is separately and relatively loosely identified in the school budget but not discussed as a coherent strategy in the headteacher/principal's termly report to governors.	Brief costed plans for improving parent partnership have been included in the School Improvement/Development Plan. The headteacher/principal makes reference to parent partnership spending as part of a coherent strategy in their termly report to governors, leading to informed questioning.	The School Improvement/Development Plan and Pupil Premium Strategy contain detailed references to the school's parent partnership strategy, costed where appropriate, and robust monitoring and evaluation processes exist, leading to rapid change where necessary and judgements about value for money when appropriate. Governors are well-informed about, and thoroughly involved in financial decisions related to, parent partnership strategies.
Notes and evidence with next steps planned:			
Strategies used to maximise parent partnership (including monitoring and evaluation)	A number of *ad hoc* but largely successful strategies are in place to improve attendance and punctuality. Some members of staff have participated in training about parent partnership. The school conducts in-school and Ofsted surveys and questionnaires to gather parent voice. Parent partnership activities are included in the School Improvement/Development Plan and the Pupil Premium Strategy. Some parents access the support offered to help their child with home learning, including links on the website. Parents are regularly encouraged by the school to support their Teachers and other school staff are aware of the need	The school is building up a coherent approach to improving and maintaining attendance and punctuality. All relevant staff have had some training in parent partnership techniques, but this has yet to reach all teachers and support staff. Annual in-school parent surveys are returned by the majority of parents and the responses are analysed and acted on. Coherent plans for developing parent partnership can be found in a variety of school documents, but evidence to evaluate impact is only beginning to be collected. Messaging about the importance of reading at home is clear and actively supported by most parents who have the literacy levels to do so. Most parents communicate confidently with school staff using a variety of means, and they generally describe staff as approachable when asked. When help with learning or wellbeing is offered sensitively, most parents respond positively and are prepared to play their	A range of tried-and-tested strategies to maximise attendance and punctuality is in place. A programme of parent partnership CPD is in place for all relevant staff, with regular updates and bespoke induction training in this area for those joining the school. The school frequently consults less-engaged parents with user-friendly methods to find out what they think would help them to become more involved. Clear, evidence-based plans are in place to achieve precise objectives, with effective monitoring, evaluation, refining and rethinking. The school provides a wide range of strategies to support learning at home which are well-used by almost all parents. Book reading is widely recognised by parents as highly beneficial and is well-supported at home, even when parents' own literacy levels are low. Summer reading is successfully encouraged by staff. Parents' self-efficacy is built by school staff treating them as equal partners, and needs-based, more sustained and intensive support is accepted by parents if appropriate. They readily access help from the school when they feel they need it, and are well-supported to set routines, foster

(continued)

(Continued)

Area of provision	Developing	Establishing	Refining
	to communicate well with all parents but find that they cannot do so with a significant group of them, who are also reluctant to accept any help offered. The school provides limited support for families' practical and economic needs. The school offers support for parenting as need arises, using a small number of relevant staff members who have the parents' trust. The school uses letters home and emails to share information with parents. Occasionally, home visits are used when the need arises, with risk assessments in place.	part in supporting any activities offered. The school is piloting a group parenting programme, with a number of staff, and perhaps parent volunteers, receiving training in its delivery. This is beginning to complement informal, one-to-one support. The school provides comprehensive support for families practical and economic needs, using such opportunities to interact with participating parents, thus developing positive relationships. An online communication platform has been chosen and is being piloted, to supplement more traditional methods such as newsletters, texts and phone calls. Home visits are used regularly by relevant staff, with safe protocols.	good home-learning habits and develop self-regulation in their children. A group-based parenting programme runs periodically with full uptake by those families who could benefit most. The school has well-embedded and widely accessed support systems for family's practical and economic needs, with parents playing an active role in delivery and signposting parents to other services if required. Efficient, effective and accessible two-way communication systems between school and home are well-used by almost all parents and staff. Where possible they are personalised, linked to learning and celebrate success. Safe home visiting by relevant staff is a proven communication and support tool.

Notes and evidence:

Appendix

| Reporting parent partnership strategies to stakeholders – e.g. parents, governors, partner services, Ofsted | Governors are informed through termly reports from the headteacher/principal about the school's general approach to parent partnership. The school's self-evaluation document makes broad references to parent partnership, and the school's website has a brief statement about its importance in relation to pupils' learning and wellbeing. Newsletters, Facebook pages and other communication platforms are used to provide limited information about parent partnership strategies used by the school. Parents are able to contact the school relatively easily, but a group of them engage less well for a variety of reasons. | Governors are fully aware of the nature and extent of parent partnership strategies through discussions at meetings, although they do not yet have sufficient data to evaluate their effectiveness. The school's self-evaluation document includes detailed references to the parent partnership actions and approaches chosen, and the website has an accessible and engaging section on parent partnership, including information about its potential impact on pupils' learning and wellbeing. Newsletters, Facebook pages and other communication platforms are used to provide comprehensive information about parent partnership strategies used by the school. Parents often contact the school when they need to, but a small group of them engage less well for a variety of reasons. | Governors are fully involved in helping to decide the nature and extent of parent partnership strategy, including evaluation of the evidence of impact, contributing to decisions made about future practice.

The school's self-evaluation document includes detailed and coherent references to the parent partnership actions and approaches chosen, and the website has a full and informative section on parent partnership, including evidence of its potential impact on pupils' learning and wellbeing. A comprehensive range of communications systems, including Facebook pages, newsletters, posters and electronic platforms, is used to inform stakeholders about all aspects of parent partnership, including a full account of the systems and activities used to encourage and enable it widely. Almost all parents engage fully with the strategies offered and readily share with the school their own ideas about them, including how they might be improved. Effective strategies are in place to overcome barriers to involvement and engagement for those families affected by them. |

Notes and evidence:

© Nigel Bishop Education Ltd 2022 *– Parent(s) refers to parent(s)/carer(s) throughout this document For more detail on strategies, visit the EEF website

IMPLEMENTING CHANGE SUCCESSFULLY – PARENT PARTNERSHIP

Creating the climate for change	Create a sense of urgency	Identify a compelling driver for making a change to practice (e.g. real frustration about current methods, Ofsted criteria).
	Form a guiding coalition	Recruit a group of willing volunteers with a variety of roles (e.g. a school leader, a teacher, a family liaison worker).
	Create a vision for change	Agree with the change group what new practice is designed to achieve and what it might look like.
Engaging and enabling the organisation	Communicate the vision and encourage buy-in	Share the new practice with the wider school, possibly through a pilot project with measurable improvements.
	Empower broad action	Cascade the successful or adapted pilot project throughout the school, with necessary changes to systems.
	Generate quick wins	Identify advantages of the new practice in terms of time saved, outcomes improved, job satisfaction, etc.
Implementing and sustaining change	Build on change (sustain momentum)	Monitor the impact regularly and develop the practice further, including the use of suggestions from practitioners and references in SEF and SIP.
	Make it part of the culture	Celebrate successes on, for example, the school website, the prospectus, and include references to it in staff and pupil induction.

© Nigel Bishop Education Ltd 2022 (Based on John Kotter's eight stages of effective change)

For Product Safety Concerns and Information please contact our EU representative GPSR@taylorandfrancis.com
Taylor & Francis Verlag GmbH, Kaufingerstraße 24, 80331 München, Germany

www.ingramcontent.com/pod-product-compliance
Lightning Source LLC
Chambersburg PA
CBHW082102230426
43670CB00017B/2924